Our

Mother

Tongue

Nancy Wilson, *Our Mother Tongue: An Introductory Guide to English Grammar*
Copyright © 2004 by Nancy Wilson
Cover design by Paige Atwood.
Printed in the United States of America.
ISBN-13: 978-1-59128-011-8
ISBN-10: 1-59128-011-7

Published by Canon Press, P.O. Box 8729, Moscow, ID 83843
800-488-2034 | www.canonpress.com

Library of Congress Cataloging-in-Publication Data
Wilson, Nancy
  Our mother tongue / Nancy Wilson.
  p. cm.
  Includes index.
  ISBN 1-59128-011-7 (Paperback)
  1. English language—Grammar—Juvenile literature. 2. English
  language—Religious aspects—Christianity—Juvenile literature. I.
  Title.
  PE1112.W556 2004
  428.2—dc21

                          2003003534

12 13 14 15 16   15 14 13 12 11

OUR MOTHER TONGUE

An Introductory Guide to English Grammar

NANCY WILSON

canonpress
Moscow, Idaho

to Duane and Joan for the years of cheerful encouragement

CONTENTS

INTRODUCTION

What is English?

We know that God Himself created language. The Bible tells us that He spoke all things into existence. God spoke to man in the garden, and we see that He also gave man the gift of language and assigned man the task of finding words suitable for naming all the creatures. Language is truly a wonderful gift. In Genesis 11:1 we learn that "Now the whole earth had one language and one speech." But due to man's rebellion at the Tower of Babel, "the Lord confused the language of the whole earth" (v. 9) so that the people could no longer understand one another. Since then, man has had to work very hard to learn the many languages of the world.

English belongs to the Germanic branch of the Indo-European family of languages. Some of the other languages in this branch include German, Dutch, and the Scandinavian languages. English grew out of other languages as well, mostly as the result of wars and invasions. English has changed so much over time that early English is difficult for many to recognize as English at all. Consider this example of Old English from the Bible: *Ne beoth ge thy forhtran, theah the Faraon brohte sweordwigenra side hergas.* This means "Be not frightened thereat, though Pharaoh has brought sword wielders, vast troops."

The Romance languages constitute another branch of the Indo-European languages, but they grew out of Latin instead of Germanic roots. The languages derived from Latin are called Romance languages because Latin was the language of Rome. These include French, Italian, Portuguese, Romanian, and Spanish. Although English is not a Romance language, over the years it acquired many words from Latin. In fact, over fifty percent of English vocabulary has Latin roots. The Romance languages can claim closer to eighty percent Latin roots. English has borrowed from many other languages besides Latin as well. I recommend the video series *The Story of English** as a fascinating overview of the

---

* A BBC documentary. Written by Robert McCrum, et al.; hosted by Robert Macneil, 9 programs on 5 VHS cassettes (Home Vision Entertainment, 1997 [1986]).

development of English. We should strive to teach our students not only to love our mother tongue and how it works, but also to love the story behind it all.

Though English has many thousands of words, each one falls into one (or sometimes more than one) of the eight categories of words, called the parts of speech. English has old or archaic words, new words, foreign words, slang, and words for every discipline or study. Each word has a history, called its etymology. Etymology is the study of words and their origins. Words are very important for the Christian because God chose to reveal Himself to man through the words of the prophets and the apostles in the Bible, and through His Son, the *logos* or Word of God, Jesus Christ. Christians should, above all others, be people of the Word, and people who love words. Writing, reading, and language should be of great interest to God's people, for by means of these tools they can know Him better and glorify Him.

The logical starting point for the study of English is the study of grammar, which is the study of the rules that govern our mother tongue. Language is much like a family with its own culture, traditions, customs, and rules. And, like a family, a language changes with time. The story of how English acquired all its peculiar customs and rules is a fascinating story in itself. Many of our grammar rules came into being in the eighteenth century when the Enlightenment inspired man to reduce everything into neat, tidy, governable systems. In many cases these rules have no particular reason for existing apart from the fact that someone loudly and authoritatively asserted them. Nevertheless, here we are now at the beginning of the twenty-first century, and we have a body of widely accepted rules to govern our speaking and writing. It is good for us to know and understand these rules without becoming slaves to them. Like the Sabbath, they should exist for us, not the other way around. This means that a good writer will sometimes break the rules, but he does so for a designed effect and not out of ignorance or laziness. Because we live in a culture that wants no rules, we Christians should desire to preserve and pass on all the important tools of communication, knowing that language is a means, not an end in itself. Language is a God-given tool for our enjoyment and enrichment. It is a gift from Him we must not squander or misuse, but rather glory in. Studying our language enables us to choose our own words wisely, to enjoy and appreciate great literature, to understand the thoughts of others, to give clear and correct expression to our own thoughts, and to train our minds to think in an orderly fashion.

Why another grammar book?

That is a good question. The world seems to be quite full of grammar books, but it is not easy to find a text today that covers all the bases, still emphasizes diagraming, is not laden with politically correct jargon, and embraces a Christian world view. I am certainly not claiming to have achieved all these things in this little book, but I have aimed for it. I wanted to produce a grammar book that could be used to teach junior-high students as well as high-school or college students and adults, a book that covered many of the aspects of English grammar succinctly; I also wanted a book that could assume the biblical view of language. At the same time I wanted to whet the appetite of the student to want to know more about the history of our language. In the classical Christian school movement, students and teachers often find that they learn more about English in Latin class than they ever did in English class. Words like *conjugation* or *predicate nominative* are new to them when they come to study Latin. I have used this book to teach what I call Refresher English to college students who are studying Latin and Greek for the first time, and to home schooling parents who need to brush up before (or while) they teach their children.

Diagraming is included and emphasized because it is a healthy review exercise that requires the student to break down the sentence, analyzing and labeling each part logically. Students generally enjoy the challenge of the diagraming. Though some may prefer to parse sentences verbally, I believe diagraming achieves the same thing with more ease, especially in a classroom setting where you want each student to analyze several sentences.

I have relied on many old and new texts to write this book. Some time ago I began collecting English grammar texts from the nineteenth century, and I have used my stash of old grammars for examples, exercises, and information. In fact, you could say there is not one original thought in the whole book. I have merely researched, arranged, collected, and organized the data. My favorite authority on the English language is H.W. Fowler's *A Dictionary of Modern English Usage.* I recommend every household have at least one copy on the shelf—it is both authoritative and entertaining. Used book stores seem to have a plentiful supply.

Of course you probably realize the shocking state of English grammar in the government schools today. One friend of mine who teaches in an elementary government school confessed to me that she sometimes shuts the door of her room and teaches grammar to her students. When one of my junior-high students (who had transferred to the Christian school from the government school) needed tutoring in grammar, his parents employed a college student over the summer. The tutor called me to find out what we would be covering in the fall. When I began by mentioning the eight parts of speech, the tutor replied, "I can't believe you still teach that stuff! What are the parts of speech again? I can't remember."

I have realized in preparing this book that a grammar book can never really be done. There is always so much more that could be researched, rewritten, improved, clarified, and explained better. I fully anticipate that those who use this book will find errors, in spite of the fact that I have gone over it repeatedly. (If you do find any, please write me so I can make the necessary corrections.) Nevertheless, my hope is that this will be of some use to those who, by the grace of God, want to employ their mother tongue to the glory of God and for the furtherance of His kingdom.

Finally, I must thank a few important people who helped me assemble this. The Logos School administrators, Tom Garfield and Tom Spencer, were very kind to give me the opportunity to teach junior-high English in the first place, and they exhibited great patience in the production of this book. My friends Tora Whitling, Katie Hurt, and Anita Evans cheerfully tested the material to see if it made any sense to moms. And I owe a debt of gratitude to Canon Press for painstakingly checking it over and over again for clarity as well as technical accuracy. Last, but most importantly, my deepest gratitude to my husband Douglas whose love for the written word and the glory of God has shaped my vision for even this humble project.

UNIT ONE

THE EIGHT CLASSES OF WORDS

Although the English language has many words, there are only eight different classes or kinds of words. Each of these classes has a definite job to do in the language. They are called the **parts of speech**. *Parts* means divisions and, of course, *speech* means language, so the **parts of speech** are simply the *divisions of language*.

CONTENTS

LESSON I

NOUNS

Examples

1. *God* controls the *history* of the *world* perfectly.

   The word *God* is the name of a person; the word *history* is the name of a thing (a field of study); the word *world* is the name of a place.

2. A Christian *student* sees the *hand* of *God* in all *events*.

   The word *student* is the name of a kind of person; the words *hand* and *events* are names of things; the word *God* is the name of a Person.

3. *Studying* with this *perspective* provides *hope* and *encouragement* for the *future*.

   The word *studying* is the name of an activity; the words *perspective* and *future* are the names of things (concepts or ideas); and the words *hope* and *encouragement* are the names of qualities or ideas.

Explanation

Man has been naming things since God gave Adam the job of naming all the animals. Naming is unique to man. It is a way that man takes dominion over the earth. Today we still name our children and our churches and schools, and man is forever coming up with naming words for new activities (*rollerblading*), new inventions (*microwave, Internet*), new discoveries (*electricity*), and new ideas (*postmodernism*). English has one class of words used to *name* things. These words name persons, places, or things that we can see; they name things that we can perceive with our other senses (such as sounds, smells, or tastes); they name qualities or ideas that we can think about (such as *beauty, mind, soul, life,* or *liberty*); or they name activities (such as *running, thinking, singing,* or *shopping*). A noun is used to name anything that exists or anything that we can think of. These naming words are called **nouns**. The word *noun* comes from the Latin word *nomen* which means *name*. A noun is always the *name* of something.

 Definition

A *noun*, or a name word, is the name of a person, place, thing, activity, or idea. *Noun* comes from the Latin *nomen,* "name."

⌛ Historia

Have you ever wondered why our language is called *English*? Because it was first spoken in England, of course! But why is England called *England*? The earliest inhabitants of England were called the Britons, a Celtic people living in southern England. The old Latin name for Britain is *Britannia*. (Only a few geographic names from the Britons' ancient tongue survive in modern English.)

The Roman general Julius Caesar invaded Britannia in 55 B.C. Though it took nearly one hundred years to complete the conquest, for the next four hundred years Britain was a Roman province, and many Latin words were introduced into the language. The Romans built roads, established camps and forts, and constructed large walls to keep out the invading Scots and Picts from the north. The most famous Roman wall is Hadrian's Wall, and its remains are visible today. Latin words introduced into the British tongue during the Roman occupation include *wall* (from the Latin *vallum*), mile (from the Latin *milia passuum*, meaning a thousand paces), and *street* (from the Latin *strata via*, meaning paved way).

When Rome began to fall to invading barbarians, the Roman soldiers were called home to help in its defense. By A.D. 410, the Romans had abandoned Britannia, leaving the country defenseless. Consequently, in the middle of the 400's, warring Germanic peoples (the Angles, Jutes, and Saxons)

Continued on next page

EXERCISE A

On a separate piece of paper, list two nouns for each of the categories below. (All exercises should be done on your own paper.)

1. Persons you have studied in history.
2. Places you would like to visit.
3. Things you use on a daily basis.
4. Qualities you admire in a friend.
5. Physical feelings (such as *pain*).
6. Mental feelings (such as *pity*).
7. Activities.
8. Subjects to study (such as *history*).

EXERCISE B

Write down all the nouns in the following paragraph (divided into sections for convenience) from *Over the Teacups* by Oliver Wendell Holmes. For each word, write down why it is a noun (for example, *tree* is a noun because it is the name of a thing—a plant). Remember that a noun names persons, places, things, activities or ideas. Be sure to look at what the word is *doing* in the sentence. Is it *naming* something?

Example. A *tree* is an underground *creature*, with its *tail* in the *air*. All its *intelligence* is in its *roots*. All the *senses* it has are in its *roots*. Think what *sagacity* it shows in its *search* after *food* and *drink*! Somehow or other, the *rootlets*, which are its *tentacles*, find out that there is a *brook* at a moderate *distance* from the *trunk* of the *tree*, and they make for it with all their *might*.

1. They find every crack in the rocks where there are a few grains of nourishing substance they care for, and insinuate themselves into its deepest recesses.
2. When spring and summer come, they let their tails grow, and delight in whisking them about in the wind, or letting them be whisked about by it; for these tails are poor passive things, with very little will of their own, and bend in whatever direction the wind chooses to make them.
3. The leaves make a deal of noise whispering. I have sometimes thought I could understand them, as they talk with each other, and that they seemed to think they made the wind as they wagged forward and back.
4. Remember what I say. The next time you see a tree waving in the wind, recollect that it is the tail of a great underground, many-armed polypus-like

creature, which is as proud of its caudal appendage, especially, in the summer-time, as a peacock of his gorgeous expanse of plumage.

Exercise C

Write five sentences of your own and underline all the nouns you use.

Common and Proper Nouns

Look at the examples below.
1. **The** *boy* **who won the prize was** *John Baker.*
   The word *boy* is a general term that is common to all young males. *John Baker,* however, is the name of a particular boy.
2. **Though I was born in a small** *town,* **I later moved to** *Chicago.*
   The word *town* is a general term, while *Chicago* is the name of a particular town.
3. **He had never seen an** *ocean* **until this summer when he saw the** *Pacific.*
   The word *ocean* is a word that names all large bodies of water, while *Pacific* is the name of a specific ocean.

Explanation

Words used to name a general class of things are called **common nouns.** *Common* means *general.* Words used to name a particular thing, distinguishing it from others in the same class, are called **proper nouns.** *Proper* comes from the Latin *proprius* which means *one's own.* (This Latin word is the root of the English word *property* as well.) A proper noun always begins with a capital letter. Your name is your own, and it is capitalized.

Exercise D

List a proper noun for each of the common nouns listed below. Remember to capitalize all proper nouns.

Example. *Street* is a common noun, but *Baker Street* is a proper noun.

1. restaurant	6. continent
2. country	7. politician
3. county	8. team
4. national park	9. store
5. teacher	10. book

Continued from previous page

began to invade. They succeeded in pushing the Britons into the northern and western parts of Britain. The Angles settled in central Britain, and the land became known as *Angle-land.* Later this became *England,* and the language spoken, our own mother tongue, became known as *English.*

■☐ *Definition*

A *proper noun* is an individual name, while a common noun is a general or class name. *Proper* derives from *proprius,* "one's own."

REVIEW QUESTIONS

1. Give the definition of a noun, and tell the Latin history of the word.
2. What kinds of things can a noun name?
3. What is the difference between a proper and a common noun?

LESSON 2

VERBS

Examples

1. Columbus *sailed* from Spain on August 3, 1492.
   The word *sailed* asserts or states something about Columbus.
2. *Did* he *lose* any of his three ships on the voyage?
   The words *did* and *lose* are used to ask a question.
3. *Read* this book about his journey.
   The word *read* is used to tell someone to do something.

Explanation

A word used to assert what a person or thing *does* or *is*, or that *asks* what a person *does* or *is*, or *tells* another person to *do* or *be* something is called a **verb**. The verb is the only word that can assert; it asserts action (even action performed by the mind, like *think*, *consider*, or *love*), condition, being, or existence. Though it is difficult to explain what a verb actually does, it is the most important word in the sentence; it is the life of the sentence, for there can be no complete sentence without a verb. The word *verb* comes from the Latin word *verbum* which means *word*.

■□ *Definition*

A *verb* is a word which can assert action, being, or existence. *Verb* derives from *verbum*, "word."

EXERCISE A

Notice in the examples below that the sentences have both naming and asserting parts.

Naming	Asserting
Man	*beholds* the face.
God	*looks* upon the heart.
Man	*considers* the actions.
God	*weighs* the intentions.

The naming parts of the sentences below are provided. On a separate piece of paper, make up some action verbs which assert (or express) what the following things do.

1. The student _____ .   6. The dentist _____ .
2. The wind _____ .   7. Airplanes _____ .
3. The desk _____ .   8. The tree _____ .
4. The clock _____ .   9. The class _____ .
5. The bus _____ .   10. The baby _____ .

Auxiliaries or Helping Verbs

■❑ *Definition*

An *auxiliary* or *helping verb* is one that is used to help another verb to assert.

Look at the italicized words in the sentences below. In each sentence the verb is comprised of more than one word.

1. **The class** *is studying* **the history of England.**

   The word *is* helps the main verb *studying*.

2. **They** *will be memorizing* **many dates and facts.**

   Will be helps the main verb *memorizing*.

3. **By the end of the semester, they** *should have covered* **much of the material.**

   Should have helps the main verb *covered*.

Explanation

A word that helps a verb to assert is an **auxiliary** or **helping verb**. When a group of words is used as a verb, it is called a **verb phrase**. However, we refer to the whole verb phrase as the verb. The following verbs are helping verbs. It will be beneficial if you memorize them. You can sing them to the tune of "London Bridge" if you would like.

Helping Verbs: *Be, is, am, are, were, was, being, been, shall, will, have, has, had, do, does, did, may, can, must, might, could, would, should.*

Exercise B

Fill in each of the blanks with a verb phrase.

1. Trees_____ in forests.
2. The grapes _____ ripe.
3. David _____ a lion and a bear.
4. The small boy _____ the window.
5. The artist _____ a picture.

EXERCISE C

The words in a verb phrase are not always in immediate succession. Notice the verb phrases in italics in the following sentences.

1. Where *do* pineapples *grow?*
2. *Have* you ever *read* <u>Pilgrim's Progress</u>?
3. Perhaps he *did* not really *disobey* me.
4. How *should* I *know* what you think?
5. We *could* hardly *hear* his speech.

Write five sentences with helping verbs and underline the entire verb phrase.

Linking Verbs

Look at the italicized words below. In each sentence, the verb is used to link or tie two words together in the sentence.

1. **The man** *is* **my father.**
   The verb *is* links *man* and *father.*
2. **The bread** *smells* **delicious.**
   The verb *smells* links *bread* and *delicious.*
3. **I** *feel* **sad about your loss.**
   The verb *feel* links *I* and *sad.*
4. **The day** *became* **rainy.**
   The verb *became* links *day* and *rainy.*

■☐ *Definition*

A verb that is used to make an assertion by joining two words is called a *linking verb.*

Explanation

A verb that is used to make an assertion by joining two words is called a **linking verb.** These verbs were first called copulative verbs from the Latin word *copula* which means *link* or *bond.* More recently we have simply called them **linking verbs.**

Learn the kinds of linking verbs:

1. "To be" verbs: *be, being, been, am, is, are, was, were.*
2. Sense verbs: *feel, sound, taste, look, smell.*
3. Others: *appears, becomes, grows, remains, seems, turn, prove, go.*

The word *is* has assertive power, but it has no real meaning of its own. In some constructions it resembles an equal sign in its meaning. One way to check if a verb is a linking verb is to substitute the word *is* or an equal sign ($=$) for the verb. If the meaning of the sentence is unchanged, the verb is indeed a linking verb. A linking verb can have helping verbs just like an action verb.

Examples.

1. Her brother *seems* lonely.

    (brother = lonely)

2. The team *remained* state champions for three successive years.

    (team = state champions)

3. Robert *drove* the car.

    (Robert ≠ car) *Drove* is **not** a linking verb.

N.B.

(N.B. is an abbreviation for *nota bene* which is Latin for *note well*, or *take careful note of what follows*.) To find out whether a word is a linking verb, substitute *is* or an equal sign.

EXERCISE D

Point out the linking and helping verbs in the following sentences. Note: To run the linking verb test on a question, rearrange the sentence to make a statement. Thus, "Are you my brother?" becomes "You are my brother." (You = brother)

1. The caterpillar will soon become a moth.
2. It seems a pity.
3. This will be a stormy night.
4. Is this an army?
5. You must be a man!

REVIEW EXERCISE A

In the following sentences identify each noun and each verb. Which sentences have linking verbs? Helping verbs?

1. Brevity is the soul of wit.
2. The boys were selling tickets to the game.
3. Cars raced by and raised clouds of dust.
4. We walked through the woods and enjoyed the colors of autumn.
5. Paint was peeling off the sides of the old barn.

REVIEW EXERCISE B

Below is an excerpt from Macaulay's *History of England* (third chapter) in which he describes the streets of London in the seventeenth century. Identify all the nouns and verbs that you can. Be sure to include helping verbs, and note if a noun is a proper noun.

1. The houses were not numbered; there would, indeed, have been little advantage in numbering them; for of the coachmen, chairmen, porters, and errand boys of London, a very small portion could read.

2. It was necessary to use marks which the most ignorant could under-stand. The shops were therefore distinguished by painted signs, which gave a gay and grotesque aspect to the streets.

3. When the evening closed in, the difficulty and danger of walking about London became serious indeed. The garret windows were opened, and pails were emptied, with little regard to those who were passing below.

4. Falls, bruises, and broken bones were a constant occurrence; for, till the last year of the reign of Charles the Second, most of the streets were left in profound darkness.

5. Thieves and robbers plied their trades with impunity; yet they were hardly so terrible to peaceable citizens as another class of ruffians.

6. It was a favorite amusement of dissolute young gentlemen to swagger by night about the town, breaking windows, upsetting sedans, beating quiet men, and offering rude caresses to pretty women.

REVIEW QUESTIONS

1. What is the definition of a verb?
2. From what Latin word does our word *verb* come?
3. What does a helping verb do? Name all the helping verbs.
4. What is the function of a linking verb? Name the three types of linking verbs and list the verbs in each category.
5. What is the test for a linking verb?
6. What is a verb phrase?

⌛ Historia

In A.D. 449 the Jutes, Angles, and Saxons invaded Britain, and over the next 150 years they drove out nearly all of the original inhabitants (Britons). After the terrible devastation of these ruthless barbarians, little was left of the Celtic or Roman civilizations. Though nearly all trace of the Jutes is lost, the Anglo-Saxon civilization and race was founded, and the new country became known as the land of the Angles and its language an early form of English, which we call Anglo-Saxon or Old English. The Britons did leave behind a few of their words such as *bog* and *glen* and *basket*.

Christianity first appeared in Britain while it was still a Roman province. In the late 500's St. Augustine arrived from France and converted the King of the Jutes, Ethelbert. Augustine built a monastery in Canterbury and sent missionaries to the northern tribes of the Picts and the Scots. The Romans sent missionaries to the Anglo-Saxons around the year 600. Words from the Latin that were adopted into the Anglo-Saxon language at this time were religious terms such as *monk* and *clerk*.

LESSON 3

ADJECTIVES

Examples

Look at the italicized words in the sentences below.

1. **The *old, tall, red maple* tree was blown over in the storm.**
   Old and *tall* and *red maple* tell us what kind or which tree.
2. ***Both* boys fished from the bridge.**
   Both tells us how many boys.
3. ***Mother's favorite* teapot fell from the table with a crash.**
   Mother's tells us whose teapot, and *favorite* tells us which teapot.

Explanation

One class of words is joined to a noun or a pronoun (see Lesson 5) to help describe, limit, or qualify its meaning. These words answer the following questions: which? what kind? how many? or whose? The word *adjective* comes from the Latin *adjectus* which means *that can add to*. An **adjective** is added to a noun or pronoun to define its meaning more exactly. These are the three categories of adjectives:

1. **Descriptive adjectives** describe or qualify (add to) the meaning of a noun: a *blue* sky, a *fat* pony, a *greasy* sandwich. To find a descriptive adjective, you just put the words *what kind of* in front of the noun. What kind of sky? *Blue* sky. *Blue* is a descriptive adjective. What kind of pony? *Fat* pony. *Fat* is a descriptive adjective.

2. **Limiting adjectives** simply point out and tell *which?* or *how many?* They point out, as in *this* book, *that* orchestra. They tell how many (*six* boys) or tell the position or order (the *first* speaker). They include the articles: *a*, *an*, and *the*.

3. **Possessive nouns and pronouns** are also used as adjectives, answering the question *whose?* In sentence 3 above, *Mother's* is a possessive noun

modifying the noun *teapot*. Because it used as an adjective, we call it an adjective and not a noun in this sentence. In the sentence, *Please give me your hand*, the word *your* is a possessive pronoun that is being used as an adjective (*whose* hand? *your* hand). (Don't worry, pronouns will be covered in detail in Lesson 5.)

Exercise A

List a few appropriate descriptive adjectives (that tell *what kind of*) for each of the following nouns.

Example. Boy: *tall, quiet, active, athletic, loud, lanky, noisy, smart, capable, honest.*

1. dog	6. friend
2. book	7. porch
3. sign	8. hill
4. teacher	9. chair
5. meeting	10. letter

▼ *Punctuation Note*

When you have more than one adjective in succession before a noun, separate them with commas. See sentence #1 at the beginning of this lesson. A comma separates the adjectives *old, tall,* and *red maple* from the noun *tree.* However, no comma is needed between *red* and *maple* because the word *maple* is commonly associated with the word *tree.* We use commas to keep things clear. If the adjectives are separated by *and,* no punctuation is needed. *The day was bright and sunny and warm.*

The Article

Observe the very common italized words in these sentences.

1. *The* **child is sick.**

The word *child* is limited by the article *the*. It is a particular child that the reader is already familiar with.

2. *A* **soldier stood at attention.**

The word *soldier* is limited by the article *a*. In this case the article makes it clear that it is an individual soldier, singled out as a representative of a class, but with whom we are not particularly familiar.

3. Man is mortal.

Man has no article because it is unlimited and applies to all mankind.

Explanation

Three little words in the adjective family are particularly hard working. These are the **articles** *a, an,* and *the*. At least one of these words appears in almost every sentence written. The word *article* comes from the Latin *articulus* which means *a little member.*

1. *The* is a **definite article** because it points to a specific person or thing. When you say, "This is *the* book," *the* refers to one particular book. The

■□ *Definition*

An *article* is an adjective that is used to limit a noun by making it definite or indefinite. The word derives from *articulus,* "little member."

definite article *the* can be used with nouns that are either singular (one) or plural (more than one). Thus, *the book* or *the books.*

2. *A* and *an* are **indefinite articles** because they do not point to a particular person or thing.

3. *An* is used before a word that begins with a vowel sound, but is shortened to *a* before a word beginning with a consonant sound. Thus, *an* automobile, *a* car. The indefinite articles can only be used with nouns of the singular number. (*A* car, not *a* cars.)

✐ N.B.

Our language is forever undergoing change. The articles are examples of such changes. *A* or *an* is a changed form of the Saxon word *ane* or *an,* which means *one. The* is a changed form of *that.*

When you say, "This is *a* way to the river," we understand other ways exist. However, if you say, "This is *the* way to the river," we may assume it is the one and only way. Although this does not seem to be of great importance at first glance, it actually can be significant. Consider the book titled *A Handbook to Literature* (by C. Hugh Holman). If it were titled *The Handbook to Literature,* we might assume that the author thought his work definitive. As it is, we sense a certain humility on the part of the author as he acknowledges his is not *the only* handbook on literature. All this is based on the choice of article.

Exercise B

Write down the appropriate article for each blank. If no article is needed, ignore the blank.

I. _____ noun is _____ name of _____ anything.

2. _____ adjective modifies _____ noun or _____ pronoun.

3. _____ word *verbum* comes from Latin and means *word.*

4. _____ commas are needed to separate _____ series of adjectives.

Exercise C

For the nouns below, provide at least one appropriate adjective for each of the questions: Which or what kind? How many? Whose?

Example. Pitcher(s): *this, red, porcelain* (what kind or which), *several* (how many), *her* (whose).

I. tree	6. bubble
2. class	7. pillow
3. mother	8. office
4. lunch	9. dollar
5. shop	I0. bush

The Proper Adjective

Some adjectives are formed from proper nouns, so they are called **proper adjectives**. For example, food from *America* (proper noun) is called *American* (proper adjective) food. Proper adjectives are capitalized.

Proper nouns: France, Egypt, Britain, Norway

Proper adjectives: French, Egyptian, British, Norwegian

Exercise D

Write a description of a common object (such as a chair, flower, knife, shell, cat, toy). After you have written your description, circle all the adjectives you used.

Exercise E

In the excerpt below from *The Story of a Bad Boy*, chapter four, by Thomas Bailey Aldrich, identify the adjectives and point out the noun each is modifying (you may skip over the articles). Note any proper adjectives. Notice how differently the passage would read without any adjectives.

1. As we drove through the quiet old town, I thought Rivermouth the prettiest place in the world; and I think so still.
2. The streets are long and wide, shaded by gigantic American elms, whose drooping branches, interlacing here and there, span the avenues with arches graceful enough to be the handiwork of fairies.
3. Many of the houses have small flower-gardens in front, gay in the season with china-asters, and are substantially built, with massive chimney-stacks and protruding eaves.
4. A beautiful river goes rippling by the town, and, after turning and twisting among a lot of tiny islands, empties itself into the sea.

Review Questions

1. Give the definition of *adjective* and the Latin word from which it is derived.
2. What questions does an adjective answer?
3. Describe the difference between descriptive and limiting adjectives.
4. How do you punctuate a succession of adjectives?
5. Explain the difference between a definite and an indefinite article.
6. What is a proper adjective?

⌛ Historia

The history of the English language has been divided into three periods. *Old English* dates from about A.D. 500-1100. The next period, called *Middle English*, was from about 1100-1485. *Modern English* dates from about 1485 to the present. By 1485 English had dropped many of its Anglo-Saxon characteristics. French influence had declined and pronunciation and word order was much like it is today. In Middle English the pronouns *thou, thy,* and *thee* were used when speaking to children or to those with whom you were well acquainted. *Ye, your, you* were used in speaking to someone considered to be your superior, or to someone with whom you were not familiar. Gradually the "polite" forms (*ye, your, you*) were used in speaking to everyone, regardless of their rank, and eventually *ye* was replaced by *you*. The odd thing about this is that today we view the use of *thou* and *thy* and *thee* as more lofty and formal, when in fact they were the common, ordinary terms of address.

UNIT 1

LESSON 4

ADVERBS

Examples

Notice how the italicized words in the following sentences are used.

1. You must work *quickly.*

The word *quickly* tells us *how* you must work.

2. She went *home.*

The word *home* tells us *where* she went.

3. She left *today.*

The word *today* tells us *when* she left.

4. The test was *very* **difficult.**

The word *very* tells us the *degree* or *extent* of difficulty.

5. He drove *too* **fast.**

The word *too* tells us the *degree* or *extent* of his fast driving. He didn't just drive fast, he drove *too* fast.

Explanation

■□ *Definition*

An *adverb* is a word used to modify a verb, adjective, or another adverb. The word derives from *ad* and *verbum,* "to a word."

Some words are added to verbs in a sentence to tell us *how, where,* or *when* something happened. These words that are added to verbs are called **adverbs.** They may also be added to other adverbs or adjectives to tell us *to what extent.* In the fourth sentence above, *very* is modifying the word *difficult.* It tells us the extent of the difficulty. *Difficult* is used as an adjective modifying *test.* In the next sentence *fast* is an adverb modifying the verb *drove,* and *too* is an adverb modifying the adverb *fast.*

The word *adverb* comes from the Latin *ad* and *verbum* which means *to a word.* Adverbs answer the questions *how? where? when? to what extent?*

1. *How?* These adverbs deal with manner: *rapidly, impatiently, slowly, joyously.*

2. *Where?* These deal with place: *here, there, home.*

3. *When?* These deal with time: *soon, late, tomorrow, today, later.*

4. *To what extent?* These deal with degree: *more, too, very, almost, quite.*
Other adverbs include those of affirmation: *yes, certainly, doubtless;* and adverbs of negation: *not, no, never.* Adverbs often convey in a single word what would generally require two or more words. The three kinds of adverbs are **simple**, **flexional**, and **phrasal.**

1. **Simple** adverbs express their meaning without an added suffix, as in the following examples: Come *here!* Pull *hard!* That is *too* bad.
2. **Flexional** adverbs are formed from all kinds of adjectives simply by adding the suffix *-ly.* Consider these examples: *quickly, slowly, snugly, loudly, hesitantly, reproachfully, cheerfully, relentlessly, sporadically, lately.* Note that adjectives already ending in *-ly,* such as *lovely* or *portly,* cannot be made into adverbs.
3. **Phrasal** adverbs are groups of words used as adverbs. These we will study in Lesson 19, and we will cover adverb clauses in Lesson 20.

Examples

Consider the examples of adverbs in each class below.

of manner (how?)	*kindly, fairly, zealously*
of place (where?)	*here, there, everywhere*
of time (when?)	*soon, today, yesterday*
of degree (to what extent?)	*almost, so, quite, too, very*
of affirmation	*yes, certainly, doubtless*
of negation	*no, not, never*
of cause (why?)	*consequently, therefore*

▼ *Punctuation Note*

When a sentence begins with the adverb *yes* or *no* (as in, *Yes, I would love to go to the concert*), it is separated by a comma from the rest of the sentence.

EXERCISE A

Write sentences following the directions below.
1. A sentence with an adverb modifying a verb.
2. A sentence with an adverb modifying another adverb.
3. A sentence with an adverb modifying an adjective.
4. A sentence with all of the above!

EXERCISE B

List all the adjectives (including articles), nouns, verbs, and adverbs in the sentence below.

The merry little man sang cheerily from the branch of a very tall tree.

EXERCISE C

Pick five verbs below and write a sentence for each using an adverb.

1. sat
2. ran
3. slept
4. read
5. wrote
6. gazed
7. skidded
8. shrank
9. shocked
10. rang

EXERCISE D

Now do the same thing for the following adjectives. *Too* and *very* are overused, so try to think of a few others.

1. pretty
2. calm
3. crowded
4. noisy
5. windy

REVIEW EXERCISE A

In the following excerpt, adapted from Washington Irving's *The Sketch Book*, identify all the nouns, verbs, adjectives, and adverbs. Do not identify articles.

1. It was a brilliant moonlit night, but extremely cold; our chaise whirled rapidly over the frozen ground; the noisy postboy smacked his long whip incessantly, and a part of the time his horses galloped.
2. "He knows he is going home," said my companion, "and is eager for some of the merriment and good cheer of the servants' hall.
3. My father is a gentleman of the old school, and takes pride in old English hospitality."
4. On our arrival, the squire came out and received us. He was a fine, healthy-looking old gentleman, with silver hair.
5. As the evening was far advanced, the squire quickly ushered us into the company, which was assembled in a large, old-fashioned hall.

REVIEW QUESTIONS

1. What is the definition of an adverb?
2. What questions does an adverb answer?
3. What distinguishes simple adverbs?

4. How are flexional adverbs formed?
5. Explain the Latin from which our word *adverb* comes.
6. How do you punctuate a sentence beginning with the adverb *yes* or *no*?

LESSON 5

PRONOUNS

Examples

1. Bill asked *me* for a cookie.

   The word *me* takes the place of the speaker's name.

2. *I* gave *him one.*

   The word *I* takes the place of the speaker's name, the word *him* takes the place of *Bill*, and the word *one* is used instead of *cookie*.

3. *He* ate *it*.

   He takes the place of *Bill*, and *it* is used instead of *cookie*.

Explanation

One class of words is used in place of a noun or a name. If we had no substitute words for nouns, our sentences would become tiresome and monotonous. Consider the sentences above and read them as they would be without pronouns. In a longer piece of writing it is even more essential that the reader is not subjected to constant repetition of names or nouns. These helpful words are called **pronouns**. The word *pronoun* comes from the Latin *pro nomen* and means *for a name*. So *pronoun* means "instead of a noun" or "for a noun." A pronoun stands for, but does not name, the person or thing it represents.

Although pronouns can be useful, they can also be confusing if not handled carefully. Imagine a student walking into a classroom and asking the teacher, "Has she given it to you yet?" Unless the teacher was a mind reader, the student would probably receive a blank stare. What is missing in the question is what is called the **antecedent**. The Latin roots of this word are *ante*, which means *before*, and *cedere*, which means *to go*. So an antecedent is a word that "goes before." The antecedent is the word the pronoun stands for. The teacher above could respond to the student with, "Give me an antecedent!" For clear writing and speaking, the word that the pronoun refers to should be obvious. In sentence two above, the pronoun *him* is clear because the antecedent is *Bill* in the previous sentence.

Much fun can be had with pronouns, as you will see in Unit 3, where we will discuss the special properties of pronouns (number, gender, case, and the other categories of pronouns, as well as pronoun-antecedent agreement).

Types of Pronouns

1. The following are called **personal pronouns** because they take the place of names of persons. Notice that *it* is a personal pronoun.
    - Pronouns used for the person(s) speaking: *I, me, myself, we, us, ourselves.*
    - Pronouns used for the person(s) spoken to: *you, yourself, yourselves.*
    - Pronouns used for the person(s) spoken of: *he, him, himself, she, her, herself, it, itself, they, them, themselves.*

2. *Myself, ourselves, yourself, yourselves, himself, herself,* and *itself* are **reflexive pronouns**. These are compound personal pronouns that are formed by adding *self* or *selves* to a personal pronoun. *Reflexive* means "back-bent." These pronouns are used to refer back to the subject of the verb, as in *I will do it myself. Myself* refers back to the subject *I,* and is used for emphasis. In other cases, the action of the verb is performed on its subject, as in *she scolded herself.* The following sentence uses the reflexive pronoun incorrectly: "She invited Mike and myself to go swimming." Here *me* should be used instead of *myself.*

3. The pronouns below are called **possessive pronouns** because they show ownership.
    - Pronouns used for the person(s) speaking: *my, mine, our, ours*
    - Pronouns used for the person(s) spoken to: *your, yours*
    - Pronouns used for the person(s) spoken of: *his, her, hers, their, theirs*

The possessive pronouns are used to answer the question *whose?* of a noun. In other words, although they are pronouns, they do the work of both a pronoun and an adjective. Some call these words pronoun-adjectives, or refer to them in a sentence as an adjective.

▼ *Punctuation Note*

Notice that possessive pronouns do not require an apostrophe, while nouns do require the apostrophe to show possession. Pronouns: *his, hers, its, theirs.* Nouns: *John's, Susan's, boy's, Mother's, family's.*

Examples

In the following sentences notice how the use of pronouns greatly improves the sentences. Also notice how the possessive pronouns modify nouns (answering the question *whose?*), but they still take the place of names or nouns.

⌛ Historia

The three Germanic tribes (Angles, Saxons, and Jutes) that invaded England in the fifth and sixth centuries A.D. are referred to as Anglo-Saxons. Old English (or Anglo-Saxon) is a combination of the dialects they spoke. Anglo-Saxon sounds a lot more like modern German than modern English. About a fifth of the words in English today are of Anglo-Saxon origin. Some people think that the King James Bible is written in Old English because it uses the old pronouns *thee* and *thou*. Actually, King James English is considered Modern English, because the King James Bible was published in 1611. Recall that the three main periods of English are Old English (500-1100), Middle English (1100-1485), and Modern English (1485-Present). To see how different Old English is from Modern English, look below at the Lord's Prayer.

Fæder ure, þu þe eart on heofonum,
Father our, thou that art in heavens,

Si þin nama gehalgod.
Be thy name hallowed.

To becume þin rice,
Arrive thy kingdom,

Gewurþe ðin willa on eorðan, swa swa on heofonum.
Be-done thy will on earth, so-as in heavens.

Urne gedæghwamlican hlaf syle us todæg
Our daily loaf give us today

Continued on next page

No pronouns: This is Susie's test that *Susie* took last week in algebra. *Susie* got an A on the *test*.

Pronouns: This is Susie's test that *she* took last week in algebra. *She* got an A on *it*.

No pronouns: Jack gave *Jack's* tickets to the game to *Jack's* mother and *Jack's mother's* friends.

Pronouns: Jack gave *his* tickets to the game to *his* mother and *her* friends.

In the following sentence from Mark 9:2, notice the use of pronouns. What nouns would have to be supplied if pronouns were not used? How would the lack of pronouns affect the sentence?

"Now after six days Jesus took Peter, James, and John, and led them up on a high mountain apart by themselves; and He was transfigured before them."

EXERCISE A

Rewrite the following sentences substituting pronouns where needed. Excessive use of pronouns can make your speech and writing confusing, so be careful to keep your pronouns and their antecedents clear.

1. Jan bought Jan a set of dishes.
2. Jan later realized that Jan did not need the set of dishes as much as Jan's sister Kate did.
3. So Jan gave Jan's set of dishes to Jan's sister Kate.
4. Kate was pleased that Jan had been so generous to Kate.

Do you see how annoyingly painful English would be without pronouns?

EXERCISE B

In the following paragraph from Genesis 41:9–15, circle all the personal pronouns including all the possessive pronouns used as adjectives. For an extra activity in this exercise, you may also notice the antecedent of each personal pronoun and tell if the pronoun is being used for the person speaking, the person spoken of, or the person spoken to.

1. Then the chief butler spoke to Pharaoh, saying: "I remember my faults this day.
2. When Pharaoh was angry with his servants, and put me in custody in the house of the captain of the guard, both me and the chief baker, we each had a dream in one night, he and I.
3. Each of us dreamed according to the interpretation of his own dream.

4. Now there was a young Hebrew man with us there, a servant of the captain of the guard.

5. And we told him, and he interpreted our dreams for us; to each man he interpreted according to his own dream.

6. And it came to pass, just as he interpreted for us, so it happened.

7. He restored me to my office, and he hanged him."

8. Then Pharaoh sent and called Joseph, and they brought him quickly out of the dungeon; and he shaved, changed his clothing, and came to Pharaoh.

9. And Pharaoh said to Joseph, "I have had a dream, and there is no one who can interpret it.

10. But I have heard it said of you that you can understand a dream, to interpret it."

What about it?

The pronoun *it* has several uses, explained below with examples.

1. ***It* can be used as a substitute for a group of words.**

When she first got her driver's license, driving to the store was a thrill; now *it* is commonplace.

2. ***It* can be used as an impersonal subject.**

It has been snowing all day.

3. ***It* can be used as an impersonal object.**

He is used to roughing *it* in the woods.

4. ***It* can be used as an expletive or exclamation.** (An *expletive* is an oath or otherwise violent or meaningless exclamation.)

What a pain *it* was to drive through all the slush!

Blast *it!*

Exercise C

Write a sentence for each of the four uses of *it* as explained above.

Review Questions

1. What is a pronoun?
2. From what Latin words does *pronoun* come, and what does it mean?
3. What is an antecedent? What Latin words are its roots?
4. List the personal pronouns used for the person speaking.

Continued from previous page

And forgyf us ure gyltas
And forgive us our debts

swa swa we forgyfað urum gyltendum.
so as we forgive our debtors.

And ne gelæd þu us on costnunge,
And not lead thou us into temptation,

Ac alys us of yfele.
but loose us of evil.

Soþlice.
Soothly (Amen).

🖋 *N.B.*

If the terms *subject* and *object* are not clear to you, they will be covered in Lessons 11, 21, and 22.

UNIT 1

5. List the personal pronouns used for the person spoken to.

6. List the personal pronouns used for the person spoken of.

7. Why are some pronouns called possessive?

8. List the possessive pronouns used for the person speaking, spoken to, and spoken of.

9. Why are possessive pronouns adjectives?

10. Do possessive pronouns require apostrophes?

11. What are the four uses of the pronoun *it*?

PREPOSITIONS

Examples

1. She sat *between* her friends *on* the bus *to* school.

 Look at the italicized words above: *between, on,* and *to.* In each case, the word italicized is used to connect words and show the relation between them. *Between* shows the connection between *sat* and *friends*; *on* shows the relation between *sat* and *bus*; and *to* shows the relation between *bus* and *school.*

2. He ran *up* the stairs *of* the bank.

 In this sentence, *up* shows the connection between *ran* and *stairs*; *of* shows the relation between *stairs* and *bank.*

3. The children ran *over* the bridge and *across* the pasture.

 Over shows the relation between *ran* and *bridge*; *across* shows the relation between *ran* and *pasture.*

Explanation

One class of words is used to connect words and to show relation between them. These words are called **prepositions.** Prepositions are generally placed before nouns or pronouns. The word *preposition* comes from the Latin *praepositus* which means *placed before.* A preposition is placed before a noun or pronoun (called the *object* of the preposition) to show its relation to some other word in the sentence. In the first sentence above, the object of the preposition *between* is *friends*; the object of the preposition *on* is *bus*; and the object of the preposition *to* is *school.* See if you can find the objects of the prepositions in sentences 2 and 3.

 In the English language we have about fifty of these relation-words. The following list includes the most used prepositions. Study this list and test your memory. Try to list (in alphabetical order) at least twenty prepositions.

■☐ *Definition*

A *preposition* is a connective word that expresses the relation of meaning between a noun or pronoun and some other word in the sentence. It derives from *praepositus,* "placed before."

aboard	at	despite	of	to
about	before	down	off	towards
above	behind	during	on	under
across	below	except	outside	underneath
after	beneath	for	over	until
against	beside(s)	from	past	unto
along	between	in	regarding	up
amid	beyond	inside	since	upon
among	*but (except)	into	through	with
around	by	near	throughout	within
			till	without

*The word *but* is a preposition when it means *except*: "All the boys *but* Bill were at the pool." When *but* is used as a connector, it is not a preposition: "I would have written, *but* I was ill." In this sentence *but* is used as a conjunction (to be covered in Lesson 7).

It is true that most of the time prepositions are followed by an object (as their name indicates, being *placed before*). However, occasionally they do appear at the end of a sentence without an object. Some grammarians insist that a sentence should never end with a preposition. However, if we apply that rule rigidly, some of our sentences will be quite awkward. Consider the following examples:

Preposition At End	**Preposition Before Object**
What did you ask for?	For what did you ask?
What are you looking for?	For what are you looking?
What are you thinking about?	About what are you thinking?
This is all I came for.	All I came for was this.
She is the one I came with.	She is the one with whom I came.

In each case above, the second sentence, though entirely correct grammatically, seems a bit rigid and formal. We should not, therefore, make our speaking or writing uncomfortable to our listeners or readers by applying this rule woodenly. Some of our best writers have contradicted this rule.

"Some little toys that girls are fond of." (Jonathan Swift)

"What god doth the wizard pray to?" (Nathaniel Hawthorne)

"Rather bear those ills we have than fly to others that we know not of." (Shakespeare)

The problem with the incorrect "Where's it at?" is not only the preposition at the end, but the use of *at* with *where* in the same sentence. The *at* on the end is entirely unnecessary. "Where is it?" is sufficient to convey the question.

EXERCISE A

Find all the prepositions in the sentences below and point out each object.

Example. *Please clean the guest room in the basement.* Preposition: *in*, object: *basement.*

1. Did you find your homework in the car?
2. After dinner they went to the theater.
3. The child sat on her lap until bedtime.
4. Besides her mother, no one else came to the recital.
5. We've had no rain since September.
6. Step into the bus quickly.
7. Without her textbook, she is lost in science class.
8. Go past the gas station and turn right on Hayes Street.
9. During dinner we had three phone calls from salesmen.
10. Throughout the winter we saw flocks of geese flying over our house.

EXERCISE B

In the groups of words below, show the relationship between the words by using appropriate prepositions. For example, in question 1 the possibilities include the sun *on* us, sun *before* us, sun *below* us.

1. sun _____ us
2. men _____ expensive cars
3. born _____September
4. light _____ Chicago
5. talk _____ computers
6. dust _____ furniture
7. asleep _____ class
8. letter _____ Aunt Leslie

REVIEW EXERCISE

In the following passage from Genesis 48:10,12-13, identify all the nouns, pronouns, verbs, adjectives, adverbs, and prepositions. Do not identify articles.

Now the eyes of Israel were dim with age, so that he could not see. Then Joseph brought them near him, and he kissed them and embraced them. So Joseph brought them from beside his knees, and he bowed down with his face to the earth. And Joseph took them both, Ephraim with his right hand toward Israel's left hand, and Manasseh with his left hand toward Israel's right hand, and brought them near him.

⌛ Historia

Old English is an inflected language. If you have studied Latin, you know what that means. In an inflected language, word order does not perform the same function as it does in other languages. For example, when we say in modern English, *God loves the world*, it matters very much which word comes first. It changes the entire meaning of the sentence if we switch the words *world* and *God* to say, *The world loves God.*

In an inflected language we understand the meaning of the sentence not by word order but by the endings of the words. In the examples above, the Latin for *God* in *God loves the world* is *Deus.* In the second sentence, *The world loves God*, the Latin word for *God* is *Deum.* One understands the meaning of the sentence not by the word order as we do in English but by the endings of the words. Modern English is no longer inflected, but it does have a few words that have kept their endings, particularly pronouns. Examples of these are *who, whom*, and *whose*, as well as *you, your*, and *yours.*

UNIT 1

REVIEW QUESTIONS

    1. Give the definition of *preposition* and its Latin roots.

    2. What is the object of the preposition?

    3. What parts of speech must the object of the preposition be?

    4. List as many prepositions as you can.

LESSON 7

CONJUNCTIONS

Examples

Some words are used to connect other words. Look at the italicized words below. Their only function is to join or connect.

1. The letter came addressed to *either* John *or* me.
2. *Both* his three ships *and* his cargo were lost on the voyage.

   The conjunctions in the above two sentences are used in pairs: *either/or* and *both/and.*
3. He eats peanut butter *and* jelly sandwiches for lunch.

   Here the word *and* connects grammatically equal words *peanut butter* and *jelly.*
4. I will type the lesson, *and* he will do the proofing.

   A conjunction can connect grammatically equal sentences. *I will type the lesson* is joined to the second sentence, *he will do the proofing,* by the word *and.* Now the two sentences are joined to form one.

Explanation

These little connecting words are called **conjunctions**. They are used to connect words, groups of words, or sentences. The word *conjunction* comes from the Latin word *conjungo* which means *to join together.* It comes from two Latin words that mean *joined* and *with.* Conjunctions come in several varieties.

   1. The most common conjunctions are *and, or, but, for, nor.* These are called **coordinating conjunctions.** They connect grammatically equal words, groups of words (called phrases and clauses*), or sentences. Look at the examples of coordinating conjunctions in the following sentences:

      - He eats cereal *or* eggs for breakfast.
      - In red coats *and* with beating drums, the soldiers came marching through town.

> ■□ *Definition*
> A *conjunction* is a word used to join or connect words, groups of words, or sentences. It derives from *conjugo,* "join together."

*Phrases, clauses, and subordinating conjunctions are covered in Lessons 16, 17, 19, and 20.

41

- He reads well, *but* his sister reads better.

Other coordinating conjunctions include

- Those which express addition: *and, also, both, as well as, further, likewise*
- Those which express separation or choice: *either, or, neither, nor, else, whether, otherwise*
- Those which express opposition: *but, yet, still, only, whereas*

2. **Correlative conjunctions** always come in pairs, and, like coordinating conjunctions, they also link words of equal importance.

> both . . . and
> not only . . . but also
> either . . . or
> neither . . . nor
> whether . . . or

3. **Subordinating conjunctions** are used to join something of less importance (a clause) to a more important element (a sentence). These will be covered later in the book.

✒ *N.B.*

Prepositions and conjunctions have similar jobs, so they should be distinguished carefully.

Although prepositions have a job similar to the conjunction in the sense that they are used to connect words, a preposition connects words that show a modifying relationship to each other. A conjunction joins two words that are to be taken together, words that grammatically are on an equal footing. The word *for* can be used either as a preposition or as a conjunction. It is important to see what function the word has in the sentence in order to determine what part of speech it is.

Preposition: He bought the book *for* the boy.

The preposition *for* shows the relationship between *book* and *boy*.

Conjunction: Please buy some cheese at the store, *for* we need it with dinner.

The conjunction *for* connects the two sentences, *Please buy some cheese* and *we need it with dinner*, making one sentence.

EXERCISE A

Write down a suitable coordinating conjunction for each blank in the following sentences.

1. He may be poor, _____ at least he is honest.
2. Sue _____ Mary are eating lunch on the lawn.
3. Either he _____ I must be wrong.
4. Hannibal, Caesar, _____ Napoleon were great generals.

5. He won the prize, _____ her essay was the best.

EXERCISE B

Supply suitable correlative conjunctions for the blanks below.

1. _____ Mother _____ Father are sick with the flu.
2. _____ Bob _____ I will take them to the doctor.
3. _____ Rachel _____ Julie were available to help.
4. Both Mother and Father have _____ a fever _____ a sore throat.
5. _____ I go _____ John goes makes no difference.

EXERCISE C

In the following sentences identify the conjunctions and tell whether they are coordinating or correlative conjunctions.

1. Both animals and plants live and grow.
2. The mother wept, for her son was dead.
3. Thomas sat down, but his little sister ran away.
4. All seek happiness, yet not all find it.
5. Neither soldiers nor sailors were available to fight.
6. Whether you go or not does not concern me.
7. They may be slow, but they are sure.
8. Either finish your supper or excuse yourself from the table.
9. He is not only ill, but he is also weak.
10. Stan as well as Dave passed the test.

REVIEW QUESTIONS

1. Give the definition of *conjunction.*
2. Give the Latin root and tell what it means.
3. What are the most common coordinating conjunctions?
4. What are the correlative conjunctions?

⌛ Historia

When we speak of the derivation of a word, we are referring to its origin. Words are divided into two general classes: **primitive** and **derivative**. A primitive word is a word that is not a changed form of an earlier word, yet it has survived to the present with no known changes. An example of a primitive word is *man.* Another word for this is *root* (the original form of a word). A derivative word is one which comes from a primitive word. Thus, we have *manly* which is derived from the primitive *man.* Consider these words derived from the root *true*: *truly, truth, truthful, untruth, untruthfulness.* Most of the derivative words in English are formed by the addition of prefixes or suffixes. Some of the prefixes of Anglo-Saxon origin are the following:

The prefix *a-* means on, in, or at. We have *a*shore (on shore), *a*sleep (in sleep).

Fore- means before. *Fore*see, *fore*tell, *fore*cast are examples.

Mis- means wrong or defective as in *mis*conduct, *mis*rule, *mis*take.

Out- means beyond or more as in *out*run, *out*live, *out*side.

With- means opposition or separation as in *with*stand, *with*draw.

LESSON 8

INTERJECTIONS

Examples

In the sentences below you see several words italicized. Each one is used to express sudden feeling or emotion and is not grammatically connected to a sentence.

1. *Oh!* I didn't know you were here.
2. *Hi!* How have you been?
3. *Welcome!* Come in.
4. *Fire! Fire!*

Explanation

■▢ *Definition*

An *interjection* is a word (or group of words) used as a sudden expression of feeling or emotion that is not grammatically connected to a sentence. It derives from *interjectus,* "thrown between."

Words used to express sudden feeling or emotion are called **interjections**. They are exclamatory words and merely express emotion; they do not form a grammatical part of a sentence. They are, in a sense, just thrown in. The word *interjection* comes from the Latin *interjectus* which means *thrown between*. Interjections can be put into three categories:

1. **Simple interjections** are words that are never used as anything else besides interjections: *Oh! Hurrah! Hey!*
2. **Secondary Interjections** are used as other parts of speech as well: *Mercy! Goodness! Nonsense!*
3. **Phrasal interjections** are groups of words used as a single interjection: *Oh my goodness! Land of Goshen! Oh boy!*

EXERCISE A

Identify the interjections in the following sentences.

1. Quiet! You should not be talking.
2. Yikes! I broke my ankle!

3. Oh! I didn't know it was you.

4. Good heavens! What a mess you've made.

5. Wow! What a beautiful day!

6. Ouch! I cut my finger.

REVIEW QUESTIONS

1. Define interjection.

2. What is the Latin root?

3. What are some common interjections?

4. Is an interjection joined grammatically to the sentence?

5. Name the eight parts of speech.

N.B.

A *particle* is a short part of speech that connects, limits, or shows relationship. These include the article, conjunction, interjection, and preposition. It can also include prefixes and suffixes.

UNIT 1

LESSON 9

REVIEW

Now that you have learned the eight parts of speech, the exercises in this chapter will serve as a review. You should be able to answer all these questions. If you cannot, go back to the appropriate chapter to review.

REVIEW QUESTIONS

Nouns:

What does the word *noun* mean? What Latin word does it come from? What is a noun? Mention ten nouns. How many and what kinds of nouns are there? What does the word *proper* mean? What is a proper noun? What does the word *common* mean? What is a common noun? Mention ten proper nouns and ten common nouns. What is meant by part of speech? How many parts of speech are there in English?

Verbs:

What does the word *verb* mean? From what Latin word is it derived? Why does it have the name "verb"? What are the three kinds of verbs? How do we recognize a linking verb? What are auxiliary verbs?

Adjectives:

What does the word *adjective* mean? From what Latin word is it derived? What is an adjective? What parts of speech can an adjective modify? What five questions does an adjective answer? Mention ten adjectives. Which adjectives are called articles? What does the word *article* mean? From what words are *an* and *the* derived? What are the two types of articles?

Adverbs:

What does the word *adverb* mean? From what Latin word is it derived? What is the difference between an adverb and an adjective? What questions does an adverb answer?

Pronouns:

What does the word *pronoun* mean? What Latin word does it come from? What is a pronoun? What is the noun called for which it stands? Why is it so called? What kinds of pronouns are there? Which are the personal pronouns? Why are they called personal?

Prepositions:

What does the word *preposition* mean? What is the Latin root? Why is it called a preposition? List twenty prepositions. What is the object of the preposition?

Conjunctions:

What does the word *conjunction* mean? From what Latin word does it come? What is a conjunction? What are the most commonly used conjunctions? What is the difference between correlative and coordinating conjunctions?

Interjections:

What does the word *interjection* mean? What is the Latin root? What is an interjection? List several interjections. What is a *particle?*

EXERCISE A

In the sentences below from Psalm 23, name the part of speech for each word. Identify articles as articles. Possessive pronouns (that do the work of adjectives) may be identified as adjectives. Any constructions that have not yet been covered in the book will appear in parentheses, so you do not need to identify them.

1. The Lord is my shepherd; I shall not want.
2. He makes me (to) lie down in green pastures.
3. He leads me beside the still waters.
4. He restores my soul.
5. He leads me in the paths of righteousness for His name's sake.

EXERCISE B

In the following sentences add an adjective to each noun and add an adverb to each verb.

Example. Students study. *Good* students study *diligently.*

1. The sun shone.
2. Boys play.
3. Leaves fall.

In the next two sentences add an adverb to each adjective, and add an adjective to each noun.

Example. The sock was dirty. The *well-worn* sock was *frightfully* dirty.

⌛ Historia

Webster's New World Dictionary estimates that about 85 percent of Anglo-Saxon vocabulary has been lost to our Modern English because of the French and Latin words that replaced them. However, the Anglo-Saxon words that did survive include most of our prepositions, pronouns, helping verbs, and conjunctions. And though they may be few in number, these little words are some of the most often used in all our speaking and writing.

Examples of the progress of our pronouns include the Anglo-Saxon *heom,* which later became *hem* in Middle English, and then was replaced by the Viking *them.* Our pronoun *I* began as *ic. Ge* in Anglo-Saxon, became *ye* in Middle English, and *you* in Modern English. *Me, us,* and *we* have been carried straight over; *ure* became *oure* and later *our* and *ours. It* began as *hit,* and *who* was originally *hwa.* The pronouns *they, their,* and *them* were brought into the Anglo-Saxon tongue by the Vikings who settled England in the 800s.

4. The substitute teacher lectured.

5. She wrote the letter on a scrap of colored paper.

Combine the following sentences using one or more conjunctions.

6. Bob was late. Eliza was late.

7. The bus hit a parked car. The bus hit several parking meters.

8. Gladys writes articles for the school newspaper. John and Andrew design the layout.

EXERCISE C

Select a paragraph from a book you are reading and try to identify as many of the parts of speech as you can. Or, look at a piece of your own writing and do the same. Notice how often you use pronouns, adjectives, and adverbs. Do you tend to use the same ones, or do you vary the modifiers you use?

EXERCISE D

Name the part of speech for each word in the sentences below. (These sentences are taken from an English grammar book published in 1854.) In sentence 11, *where* is an adverb introducing an adjective clause; *though* in sentence 13 and *because* in 14 are both subordinating conjunctions. These words are marked with an asterisk and are covered later in the book.

1. James writes very well.

2. The Apostles preached the gospel.

3. Jesus Christ was rich, yet He became poor.

4. The Scriptures teach love to God and man.

5. Good and wise men make valuable friends.

6. A wise son hears the instructions of a father.

7. Envy and anger cause great pain, and they shorten life.

8. Anger rests in the bosom of wicked men.

9. A good man dismisses all unkind feelings.

10. Death to good men is the gate of Heaven.

11. A hospital is a place where* sick persons are received.

12. A thoughtful mind will find instruction in all things.

13. God has shown love to man, though* man returns it not.

14. We defer repentance to some future time, because* we love sin.

15. In books we find much valuable instruction.

UNIT TWO

THE SENTENCE

Syntax is the way words are arranged to make correct sentences and includes the rules of composition. Syntax is thus very important for communication—to be clearly understood, we must arrange our words in a logical manner. This unit covers the different kinds of sentences and the different components of sentence construction. Syntax is simply *sentence-making*.

CONTENTS

LESSON 10
KINDS OF SENTENCES

Examples

1. **Fire burns.**

   In this sentence, something is named (*fire*), and something is said about the fire (it *burns*).

2. **Rain is falling.**

   Something is named (*rain*), and something is said about the rain (it *is falling*).

3. **The boy was whistling loudly.**

   Something is named (*boy*), and something is said about the boy (he *whistles loudly*).

Explanation

Look at the sentences above. What is it that makes each one a **sentence** and not a random bunch of words thrown together? A **sentence** expresses a complete thought, not a partial thought. *The light in the window* is a group of words that expresses only a partial thought. Nothing is being said about the light in the window. We might convert the words into a sentence by saying, *The light in the window woke up the sleeping boy.*

EXERCISE A

Supply words that will convert the following incomplete collections of words into complete sentences.

1. In 1492 Columbus _____.
2. The state of Idaho _____.
3. A group of college students _____.
4. The large plaid tablecloth _____.
5. The Christmas tree _____.
6. _____ was a great man.

■☐ *Definition*

A *sentence* is a combination of words expressing a complete thought.

▼ *Punctuation Note*

The first word of every sentence always begins with a capital letter.

7. _____ is my favorite dessert.

8. _____ lives in Africa.

9. _____ travels frequently.

10. _____ strikes on the hour.

Kinds of Sentences

▼ *Punctuation Note*

A declarative or imperative sentence is closed with a period (.); an interrogative sentence is closed with a question mark (?); and an exclamatory sentence is closed with an exclamation point (!). If an imperative is uttered with strong emotion, it can be closed with an exclamation point also, as in *Shut the door!*

The four types of sentences are **declarative**, **interrogative**, **imperative**, and **exclamatory**.

1. **Declarative:** This is a sentence that simply expresses a statement or declares something. Examples: *The birds sing. Boise is the capital of Idaho.* Declarative sentences are *statements.*

2. **Interrogative:** This is a sentence that asks a question as in the following examples: *Are you ill? Did you hear that noise?* Interrogatives are *questions.*

3. **Imperative**: An imperative sentence expresses a command: *Pick up your sock. Answer the door.* Imperative sentences are *commands.*

4. **Exclamatory:** This is a sentence that expresses strong emotion. *I'm so happy you came! What a wonderful occasion!* When a sentence begins with the words *how, why,* or *what,* and it is not framed as a question, often it will be an exclamatory sentence. *How lovely you look! Why George! What a night it is!* Exclamatory sentences are *exclamations.*

✒ *N.B.*

Know the four types of sentences and be careful to distinguish them in your reading.

It is very important to distinguish between types of sentences. For example, when a Christian reads his Bible, he must pay close attention to the imperatives, for these are commands from God. He must also not confuse the declarative sentences with the imperatives, for declarative statements are not meant to be obeyed but believed. For example, *Believe on the Lord Jesus Christ* is an imperative. God tells us to believe. *Rejoice in the Lord always* is another imperative. This is a command to *do* something, in this case, rejoice. *God is love* is a declarative statement. This is not something we should do; rather it is something we are to believe as true.

Exercise B

Identify the sentences below as declarative, interrogative, imperative, or exclamatory and supply the appropriate end marks.

1. The farmers are harvesting the wheat

2. Tell me what you are thinking

3. Where are you going after class

4. How dark the sky is

5. Call my brother back

6. My locker is very full of books

7. His birthday is next month

8. What is the answer to question number four

9. Be quiet

10. What a day I've had

EXERCISE C

Arrange each of the following statements to form a question, a command, and an exclamation.

Example. Dogs love to bark and bite. (Statement)

Do dogs love to bark and bite? (Question)

Let the dogs love to bark and bite. (Command)

How the dogs love to bark and bite! (Exclamation)

1. The bonfire burned brightly.

2. The morning flew by.

3. The wind blew fiercely.

4. The students read eagerly.

5. The wedding was lovely.

REVIEW QUESTIONS

1. Define *sentence.*

2. What are the four types of sentences and what does each do?

3. How is each of the four types of sentences punctuated?

4. What is *syntax*?

LESSON 11

THE SUBJECT

Examples

Look at the sentences below. In each sentence something is *named,* and then something is *said or asserted about* what was named.

1. Lions roar.

In this sentence something is being asserted about *lions.*

2. Dark clouds gathered.

Something is being said about *clouds.*

3. My morning was busy.

In this sentence the thing named is *morning.*

4. He is my brother.

Something is being said about *he.*

Explanation

■☐ *Definition*

A *subject* of a sentence is the naming part about which something is being asserted or stated.

Every sentence, no matter how short or long it is, must have two parts: the naming part, which is called the **subject**; and the asserting part, which is called the **predicate.** (The predicate will be covered in the next lesson.) The **subject** of a sentence will always be a noun or pronoun. In the first three sentences above, the subjects are all nouns: *lions, clouds, morning.* In the last sentence the subject is *he,* a pronoun. Sometimes it is easier to find the verb first and then ask *who?* or *what?* before the verb. For example: *Joe ran.* The verb is *ran.* Who ran? *Joe* is the subject.

Exercise A

In the following sentences identify the subject.

1. A band was playing in the park.
2. The football game was canceled.
3. She showed me her photographs.

4. We rode home.

5. The sunset was glorious.

A sentence can have more than one subject, as in the following sentence: *Bob and Mary planted a hedge.* The subject of the sentence in this case is *Bob* and *Mary.* When a sentence has two or more subjects (as in the exercise below), the subject is a **compound subject**.

Exercise B

In the following sentences identify the subjects. Remember that the subject can be found if you ask what or who is named in the sentence, and something must be asserted or stated about that person or thing. Some of the sentences below have compound subjects.

1. Dogs and cats are America's favorite pets.

2. The students and parents gathered for school orientation.

3. My shelf is full of my favorite books.

4. *Robinson Crusoe* and *Pilgrim's Progress* are among them.

5. Ketchup, mayonnaise, and mustard were served with the hamburgers.

Exercise C

Do not assume that the subject is always at the beginning of the sentence. Sometimes it is in the middle or at the end.

Examples.

After the rain, *I* walked to the library. (The subject is *I.*)

Where do *pineapples* grow? (The subject is *pineapples.*)

Across the street and down the alley rolled the *ball.* (The subject is *ball.*)

In the following sentences identify the simple or compound subjects.

1. At the doorstep on summer evenings sat the little stray dog.

2. A noun or a pronoun can be used as a subject.

3. Adjectives and adverbs are called modifiers.

4. Up into the clouds went the balloon and string.

5. What bright blue eyes she has!

6. In the dark shade of the forest stands an old house and a weather-beaten barn.

7. Are Sue and David coming to dinner tonight?

8. Three little girls were giggling in the corner.

9. Sam and Judy will be here soon.

10. Latin and literature are his favorite classes this year.

■ Definition

A *compound subject* acts as one subject in the sentence and is made up of two or more individual subjects.

⧗ Historia

The earliest written English history is *The Ecclesiastical History of the English People*, written in Latin (*Historia Ecclesiastica*) in 731 by the scholarly monk Bede. He begins with the Roman invasion of England and describes the spread and development of Christianity in England up to his day. This work was copied and read widely in Europe. During the reign of King Alfred the Great (871-899), it was translated into Anglo-Saxon. Wanting to improve and revive the education of his people and because so few knew Latin, Alfred oversaw the translation of many important works into Old English. In fact, some of them he translated himself. These works included a book for the bishops about their pastoral duties, other religious and philosophical works, and the first fifty psalms. Because King Alfred saw the importance of preserving his country's history, he also commissioned the writing of the *Anglo-Saxon Chronicle*, a year-by-year account of the king's military defense against the invading Vikings.

UNIT 2

Exercise D

Compose five sentences of your own, two in which the subjects come last, two with the subjects in the middle, and one with the subject at the beginning.

The Understood Subject

Definition

An *understood subject* is not included in the sentence but is assumed. It is usually found in imperative (commanding) sentences.

Sometimes the subject is not included in the sentence because it is understood. Example: *Take the dog on a walk.* The subject is *you.* When the subject is understood, it is referred to in parentheses. *(You) Take the dog on a walk.* This is especially common with imperative sentences.

Consider the following excerpt from Psalm 141. The subject, *Lord,* is identified in the first part of verse 3, but it is understood to be the Lord in the latter section of the verse, as well as in verse 4.

[3]Set a guard, O Lord, over my mouth;
Keep watch over the door of my lips.
[4]Do not incline my heart to any evil thing,
To practice wicked works
With men who work iniquity;
And do not let me eat of their delicacies.

Exercise E

Write two sentences with understood subjects.

Review Questions

1. What is the definition of the word *subject*?
2. What kinds of sentences require a subject?
3. What parts of speech can be used as subjects?
4. Where is the subject found in the sentence?
5. How do you find the subject of a sentence?

LESSON 12

THE PREDICATE

Examples

1. **Birds fly.**

   In this sentence the subject is *birds*. What is being said about them? They *fly*.

2. **The storm rages.**

   Here the subject is *storm*. What is being asserted about the storm? It *rages*.

3. **I bought groceries.**

   The subject is *I*. What is being said about the subject? I *bought groceries.*

Explanation

In any sentence more is needed than just a subject. Something must be said, stated, or asserted about the subject. This is called the **predicate**. The word **predicate** comes from the Latin word *praedicatum* and is related to the word *preach*. It is the part of the sentence that is doing the "preaching," so to speak, about the subject. The simple **predicate** is always a verb. The complete **predicate** includes all the other words associated with the verb. This will become clear in subsequent lessons. For now, it is only important to understand that the verb does the asserting, and the **predicate** is simply a term to refer to the part of the sentence that is doing the asserting.

EXERCISE A

Supply suitable predicates for the following subjects.

1. London
2. The school
3. The kindly old man
4. The stormy afternoon
5. Ships

■□ *Definition*

The *predicate* is the word or words that assert or state something about the subject. It is derived from *praedicatum*, a form of *praedico*, which means to proclaim, preach, or assert.

Exercise B

Supply suitable subjects for the following predicates.

1. _____ is the season of warm days and cool, crisp nights.
2. _____ lived alone on a desert island.
3. _____ sailed across the Atlantic.
4. _____ graded papers all afternoon.
5. _____ listened eagerly to the news report.

Diagraming

Diagraming sentences is a good exercise because it forces the student to analyze every word in the sentence by examining the function of each word. Diagraming is a great way to review principles we have already learned as we continue to learn new ones. As we study the different parts of the sentence, we will diagram them. We will begin by diagraming the subject and the verb (or simple predicate). A verb phrase, which includes the verb and any helping verbs is placed on the right side of the line, like this:

Examples.

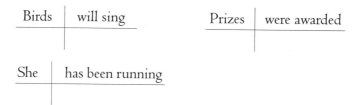

Exercise C

Diagram the subjects and verbs in the following sentences.

1. Dogs growl.
2. Boys are watching.
3. Teams are competing.
4. Houses have been built.
5. I am studying.

EXERCISE D

If a sentence has a compound subject or compound verb, the diagram is structured differently. For the sentences *Bill and Jack are racing* and *Bill and Jack are diving and racing*, the diagrams look like this:

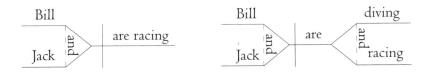

Diagram the compound subjects and compound verbs in the following sentences.

1. Poplars and willows were planted.
2. Dave and Jill are touring and traveling.
3. Mom and Dad are walking and jogging.

REVIEW QUESTIONS

1. What does the predicate do in the sentence?
2. Define the word *predicate*.
3. What two elements are needed to make a sentence?
4. What is the Latin root word for *predicate*?
5. To what other English word is it related?

LESSON 13

THE SUBJECT MODIFIED BY AN ADJECTIVE

Examples

1. *Two beautiful* **ladies danced.**

   In this sentence *beautiful* modifies *ladies*, which is the subject of the sentence. *Beautiful* tells us what kind of ladies. *Two* also modifies the subject, telling us *how many* ladies.

2. *The rainy, cold* **days have come.**

   The is an article modifying the subject *days*; *rainy* and *cold* are both modifying the subject, telling us *what kind* or *which* days.

Explanation

A subject of a sentence, because it will always be a noun or a pronoun, can be modified by one or more adjectives. Review the questions that an adjective can answer. *Which? What kind? How many? Whose?*

EXERCISE A

Combine each group of statements into one sentence, using all the adjectives to modify the subject.

Example.

The salesclerk spoke sharply to the customer. She was a *grumpy* salesclerk. She was an *impatient* salesclerk. She was a *rude* salesclerk.

Combined sentence: The rude, impatient, grumpy salesclerk spoke sharply to the customer.

1. Her garden has many visitors in the spring. Her garden is *lush*. Her garden is *fragrant*. Her garden is *colorful*.
2. The patio is behind the house. The patio is *small*. The patio is *secluded*. The patio is *shady*.

3. Now you compose two more sentences with three adjectives modifying the subject.

Exercise B

Review the punctuation note on page 25 and provide commas in the proper places in the following sentences.

1. She has an old old necklace that was her grandmother's.
2. Sam wrote a clear precise intelligent essay that won him the prize.
3. His classmates viewed him as reserved and proud ambitious and haughty.
4. The tired drooping hungry preschoolers toddled off the bus.
5. He drove a shiny new bright red pickup in the parade.

Diagraming

When a subject is modified by an adjective, the modifier is placed on a slanted line underneath the subject as in the example below. If several modifiers are used, they are all placed in the same manner, below the noun they modify. Articles are treated the same way.

Example. The bashful young girl blushed.

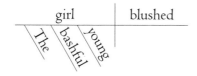

Exercise C

Diagram the following sentences.

1. His old family Bible was treasured.
2. Several favorite passages were underlined.
3. All the important family dates were recorded.
4. The black leather cover was cracking.

⏳ Historia

Anglo-Saxon poetry was used to preserve history and tradition. The oral poet or *scop* was an important member of the society who helped to keep the community together by reciting its history in poetry or song. Scholars believe the master poet composed poetry on the spot, as soon as an important feat or battle was accomplished, not only to delight an audience, but also to preserve and record the event. The poetry was oral, not written, sung not read. *Beowulf* was most likely composed by a Christian poet sometime between 650-850, but the surviving copy is from about the year 1000. It is written in a West Saxon dialect and consists of 3,200 lines, making it one of the earliest poems of considerable length in a modern language. Many of the characters in Beowulf are identified in other works, and it is probable that the events recorded occurred in the early sixth century.

UNIT 2

LESSON 14

THE SUBJECT MODIFIED BY A POSSESSIVE NOUN

Examples

1. *Mom's* pies are famous.

    The proper noun *Mom* is used to modify *pies*, telling us *whose* pies.
2. The *school's* colors are blue and white.

    The noun *school* is used to modify *colors*, telling us *which* colors.
3. The *book's* cover was torn and dirty.

    The noun *book* is used to modify *cover*, telling us *what kind* of cover.

Explanation

■□ *Definition*

A *possessive* noun shows ownership.

A noun can be used to modify another noun (in this case the subject) by adding an apostrophe and the letter *s*. This form of the noun is called the *possessive* because it is showing possession or ownership. The possessive noun is doing the work of an adjective, because it is modifying another noun, so we can simply call it an adjective. Here are some rules to follow when forming the possessive:

1. When the word is singular (meaning one, as in a *cat*), the possessive is formed by adding apostrophe and *s*, as in *cat's*. The only exception: certain words used with *sake*, as in "for conscience' sake" or "righteousness' sake" or "appearance' sake".
2. When the word is plural (meaning two or more, as in *cats*), the possessive is formed by adding the apostrophe to the plural form: *cats'*.
3. Sometimes the plural form does not end in *s*, as in *oxen* or *children*. Then the possessive is formed the same way it is for singular, by adding *'s*. Examples: *oxen's*, *children's*.
4. With a proper noun ending in *s*, the possessive is formed by adding the apostrophe and *s*, as in *Jones's* book, *Dickens's* characters. Plural: *Joneses'*

house, *Lucases'* lands. The only exceptions are the names *Jesus* (in *Jesus'* day) and *Moses* (*Moses'* sister), and ancient Greek names (of more than one syllable) that end in *es* or *us* like *Socrates* or *Odysseus*. Only an apostrophe is added: *Odysseus'* dog, *Socrates'* writings. These are not pronounced with an extra syllable. *Jesus'* still has two syllables, not three.

Exercise A

Form the possessive for the following nouns.

1. Child, prince, baby, teacher, uncle.
2. Father, cat, John, dog, mercy.
3. Bible, verse, painter, sister, house.
4. Charles, Jesus, princess, bridge, foxes.
5. Williamses, Xerxes, Davis, geese.

Diagraming

When diagraming a possessive pronoun, it is placed the same way as any adjective, on a slanting line under the noun it modifies.

Example. Betty's dog was found.

LESSON 15

THE SUBJECT MODIFIED BY AN APPOSITIVE

Examples

1. My favorite Puritan author, *Thomas Watson,* was a great and effective preacher.

   The subject of the sentence is the noun *author.* The name *Thomas Watson* explains which author.

2. Moby Dick, *the great white whale,* is a famous character in American literature.

   The subject *Moby Dick* is identified as *the great white whale.*

3. Jonathan, *our neighbor's son,* mows our lawn.

   The subject *Jonathan* is identified as *our neighbor's son.*

Explanation

■□ *Definition*

An *appositive* is a noun which follows another noun and explains or identifies it.

When a noun that refers to the same person or thing is placed beside another noun to explain its meaning, the noun is said to be in *apposition* with the word it explains. The **appositive** is the noun that follows another noun to explain or identify it. The appositive, being a noun, can also have modifiers attached to it. The entire expression is called the **appositive phrase.** (Phrases will be covered in detail in the next lesson.) Though the appositive usually follows the word it modifies, it can sometimes precede it.

Exercise A

Identify the appositives and appositive phrases in the sentences below.

1. David, the psalmist, was a man after God's own heart.
2. Our faithful dog, a golden retriever, guards the house.
3. My father, a veteran of World War II, has several medals for heroism.
4. A fine student and leader, Sam will go places.
5. My daughter Sarah is my best friend.

EXERCISE B

Insert commas to set off the appositives as they are needed in the sentences below.

1. Mr. Gibbs the new science teacher will speak at the assembly today.
2. The new library a beautiful brick building will be quite an asset to the community.
3. The boys' piano teacher Mrs. Williams will come for supper tonight.
4. Latin a language considered dead by many people is the source of over half of English vocabulary.
5. Jim Miller the new boy on the team came from Texas.

▼ *Punctuation Note*

The appositive or appositive phrase is set off from the other parts of the sentence by commas unless the appositive is a single word closely connected to the word it explains. For example, in the sentence *My brother Bob is a physician, Bob* is the appositive, but there is no need to place commas around it.

Diagraming

When diagraming, the appositive is placed in parentheses after the word it identifies or explains. If the appositive has modifiers, they are placed beneath it just like adjectives

Example. *Moby Dick, that great white whale, destroyed the ship.*

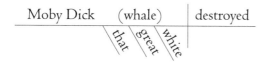

The phrase "the ship" is not included on the diagram because it is a *direct object*, which we will not cover until Lesson 21.

EXERCISE C

Diagram the following sentences with appositives.

1. My favorite book, *Pride and Prejudice*, has been reviewed.
2. The library, an old historic building, will be demolished.
3. Her puppy, a chocolate lab, is barking.

LESSON 16

THE SUBJECT MODIFIED BY AN ADJECTIVE PHRASE

Examples

1. The trees *in the park* are one hundred years old.

   Which trees? The ones *in the park.* The phrase *in the park* modifies the subject *trees. In* is a preposition and its object is the noun *park.*
2. The hat *with the large red roses* belongs to my aunt.

   What kind of hat? A hat *with large red roses.* The preposition *with* begins the prepositional phrase, and its object is *roses.* The phrase is modifying the subject *hat.*
3. The bridge *by my house* is falling down.

   Which bridge? The one *by my house. By* is the preposition, and its object is the noun *house.* The phrase is modifying the subject *bridge.*

Explanation

■❑ *Definition*

A *phrase* is a group of related words used as a single part of speech. A phrase does not contain both a subject and a verb.

A group of related words that modifies a noun or a pronoun is called an **adjective phrase.** Notice that each of the phrases above begins with a **preposition.** A prepositional phrase is a group of words that begins with a preposition and includes its object, which is usually the last word in the phrase. A prepositional phrase that modifies a noun is an **adjective phrase.** It answers the same questions an adjective answers. Do you remember those questions? *Which? What kind? How many? Whose?*

Many phrases are simply a preposition and a noun (the object of the preposition). These short phrases could be changed into single adjectives.

Examples.

   The dog *with long ears* = the *long-eared* dog (adj.)

68

The man *in uniform* = the *uniformed* man (adj.)

A vacation *for three weeks* = a *three-week* vacation (adj.)

EXERCISE A

Change the italicized adjectives into adjective phrases.

1. The storm blew down a *neighborhood* barn.
2. An *oak* table fills the dining room.
3. *Virtuous* women are pleasing to God.
4. We listened to an *historical* speech.
5. She is a *sensible* woman.

EXERCISE B

Identify the *adjective phrases* and the nouns they modify.

1. A house of stone is not uncommon in England.
2. A tourist from Australia visited us last week.
3. Roads in the country are muddy in the spring.
4. Grapes from California make fine wine.
5. The car with the broken headlight is mine.

EXERCISE C

Now you compose five sentences with adjective phrases modifying the subject.

▼ *Punctuation Note*

When a sentence has a series of introductory prepositional phrases, they are followed by a comma. For example, "After the ride through the woods on horseback in the moonlight, we were relieved to find our accommodations." "Despite many years of hard missionary work in Bolivia, the couple remained healthy and fit."

UNIT 2

Diagraming

A prepositional phrase is diagramed beneath the word it modifies. The preposition is placed on a slanted line beneath the word it modifies. This line is connected to a horizontal line on which the object of the preposition is placed. (Note that the tail of the slanted line extends just beyond the horizontal line.) Adjectives modifying the object are placed below the object on slanting lines.

Example. The steep slope of the bank was sliding.

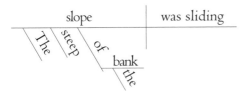

EXERCISE D

Diagram the following sentences.

1. The princess from a faraway land was kidnaped.
2. A prince on a white stallion arrived.
3. His kind offer of rescue was accepted.

LESSON 17

THE SUBJECT MODIFIED BY AN ADJECTIVE CLAUSE

Examples

1. My literature instructor, *who studied in Rome,* is also a Latin scholar.

    Which instructor? The one *who studied in Rome.* The group of italicized words modifies the subject *instructor.*

2. The book *that belongs to the library* is due tomorrow.

    What kind of book? *That belongs to the library.* The italicized words modify the subject *book.*

3. Our town's swimming pool, *which was built in 1950,* was renovated last summer.

    Which was built in 1950 modifies the subject *pool.*

Explanation

A group of related words that contains a verb and its subject, but cannot stand alone to express a complete thought, is called a **subordinate clause.** The word *subordinate* means of lesser importance. A sentence can stand alone. A subordinate clause cannot.

When a subordinate clause is used to modify a noun or pronoun, it is an **adjective clause.** Notice in the sentences above that each adjective clause in italics has a verb and its subject; however, none of the clauses could stand alone as a complete sentence. An adjective clause will usually begin with a relative pronoun: *who, whose, whom, which,* or *that.* These pronouns are called *relative* because they *relate* directly to a preceding word and connect it to the clause. *Which* is used to refer to things; *who* refers only to persons; *that* can refer to persons or things.

Examples.

He bought the car *which* was my uncle's.

He bought the car *that* was my uncle's.

■□ *Definitions*

A *clause* is a group of words that contains a subject and verb. A *subordinate clause* is a clause that cannot stand alone as a sentence. An *adjective clause* is a subordinate clause used as a single adjective.

71

She is the girl *who* lives next door.
She is the girl *that* lives next door.

✒ N.B.

Adjective clauses should be placed next to the word they modify to keep the meaning clear.

In the examples at the beginning of this lesson, each adjective clause directly follows the word it modifies. This is very important. The adjective clause must be placed next to the word it modifies to keep the meaning clear. Consider sentence 3 above. If it were written *The swimming pool in our town, which was built in 1950, was renovated last summer*, the meaning would be unclear. Was it the town or the swimming pool which was built in 1950?

Exercise A

Each of these sentences from Proverbs has at least one adjective clause. Identify both the adjective clause and the noun being modified. Also note the relative pronoun introducing the clause.

1. He who heeds the word wisely will find good. (16:20)
2. There is a way that seems right to a man, but its end is the way of death. (16:25)
3. He who has knowledge spares his words, and a man of understanding is of a calm spirit. (17:27)
4. Better is the poor who walks in his integrity than one who is perverse in his lips, and is a fool. (19:1)
5. Blows that hurt cleanse away evil. (20:30)

Exercise B

Compose five sentences with adjective clauses. Be sure to use the relative pronouns *who, whose, whom, which,* or *that*.

✒ N.B.

Sometimes adjective clauses begin with an adverb.

Sometimes adjective clauses do not begin with relative pronouns but with an adverb. For example, *This is the town* where *I grew up*. *Where I grew up* is modifying *town*. (Place/*where*) Or, *This is the time* when *we serve coffee*. *When we serve coffee* is modifying *time*. (Time/*when*) And finally, *You are the reason* why *I come home*. *Why I come home* modifies *reason*. (Reason/*why*) Also, sometimes the relative pronoun is understood, so it is omitted. *This is the prize (that) I won*.

Exercise C

Identify the adjective clauses in the sentences below.

1. This is the room where we will have the reception.

2. Here is the book I bought.

3. That is the reason why I am late.

4. May is the month when he will graduate.

5. Now is the time when we should go.

Diagraming

To diagram a sentence with an adjective clause, simply diagram the clause by itself on a line beneath the main sentence. Join the relative pronoun to the word it modifies in the sentence with a broken line. The relative pronoun will serve some grammatical function in the clause. It may be used any way that a noun can be used, as the subject, an object of a preposition, etc.

Example. *She who listens will understand.* (*Who* is the subject of the adjective clause.)

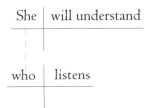

Note: Sometimes the relative pronoun is left out of the sentence. In that case it is understood.

Example: The gift [that] I ordered arrived today.

EXERCISE D

Diagram the sentences below.

1. The package that is in the hall is moving.

2. The vase which fell shattered.

3. The town that I grew up in has been abandoned.

4. The boy who laughed was corrected.

▼ *Punctuation Note*

When an adjective clause is essential to the meaning of the sentence, no commas are needed to set it off. However, if it is nonessential, it is enclosed in commas. **Examples.**

This is the day that the Lord has made. No comma is needed because *that the Lord has made* is essential to the meaning of the sentence. *This is the day* would not mean much by itself.

My cousin, who is my best friend, was born is Wisconsin. The clause is not essential (*My cousin was born in Wisconsin* can stand alone), so it is enclosed with commas.

LESSON 18

THE PREDICATE MODIFIED BY AN ADVERB

Examples

1. **The relay team ran** *remarkably well.*

   The subject of this sentence is *team.* The verb is *ran.* The adverb *well* modifies *ran,* telling how the team ran. *Remarkably* is another adverb, modifying *well.* It tells us how *well.*

2. **Today I will go home.**

   The subject of this sentence is *I.* The verb is *will go. Today* tells us when and *home* tells us where I will go. They are both adverbs modifying the verb.

3. **Some trees grow** *very slowly.*

   The subject is *trees;* the verb is *grow. Slowly* is an adverb that tells us how the trees grow, and *very* modifies *slowly,* telling us the degree or extent of the slowness.

Explanation

Adverbs can modify the verb (or predicate) in the sentence. Remember the words *not* and *never* are adverbs. They will often appear in the middle of a verb phrase, as in *You may* not *come* or *He may* never *come.* The verb in both sentences is *may come. Not* and *never* are adverbs modifying the verbs.

EXERCISE A

In the sentences below identify the adverbs that modify the verb.

1. I politely but firmly told the salesman I was not interested.
2. He resolutely continued with his sales pitch.
3. I calmly told my daughter the news.
4. He said he would call tomorrow, but he never did.
5. She is climbing down now.

Diagraming

The adverb in a sentence is diagramed the same way an adjective is diagramed: it is placed on a slanted line under the verb, adverb, or adjective it modifies.

Example. She will arrive tomorrow.

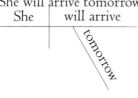

When an adverb modifies an adjective or another adverb, place it under the word it modifies.

Example. He ran very fast.

EXERCISE B

Diagram the sentences below. Place any adverbs or adjectives under the words they modify.

1. The small child cried angrily.
2. The bright yellow daffodils were blooming cheerily.
3. Several small boys were playing noisily.
4. The rustic cabin was surprisingly abandoned.
5. Today he suddenly left.

⌛ Historia

Caedmon is considered the first Christian poet in England. Bede, the author of *The Ecclesiastical History of the English People*, records the legend surrounding him. One night at a feast, the harp was being passed around for each person to take his turn to sing. Caedmon could not sing, so he excused himself from the feast and went out to take his turn with the sheep. He dreamed that a man asked him to sing, and he replied that he could not sing. But the man commanded Caedmon to sing about creation. Then Caedmon began to sing, and from then on he had the extraordinary gift of composing religious songs in meter on the spot. Caedmon showed his gift to his superiors the following day, and the abbess of the monastery charged him to become a monk. She had him instructed in "the whole course of sacred history" so that he could compose songs about all God's works. Bede records the words of Caedmon's hymn for us.

Now we must praise the Maker of the heavenly kingdom,
The power of the Creator and His counsel,
The deeds of the Father of glory and how He,
Since He is the eternal God,
Was the Author of all marvels and first created the heavens
As a roof for the children of men and then,
The almighty Guardian of the human race,
Created the earth.

THE PREDICATE MODIFIED BY AN ADVERB PHRASE

Examples

1. The Bible was written *for our benefit.*

   Why was it written? *For our benefit.* This phrase is modifying the verb *was written.*

2. It was obviously inspired *by God.*

   How was it inspired? *By God.* This phrase modifies the verb *was inspired.*

3. *Over the years* many men have laid down their lives defending the Scriptures.

   When have men laid down their lives? *Over the years.* This phrase modifies the verb *have laid.*

4. The Bible is read *in many countries* around the world.

   Where is the Bible read? *In many countries.* The phrase modifies the verb *is read.*

Explanation

■□ Definition

An *adverb phrase* is a phrase used in the sentence as a single adverb.

A prepositional phrase used as an adverb is an **adverb phrase.** Remember, just like an adjective phrase, an adverb phrase will begin with a preposition and end with its object, a noun or pronoun. In the first sentence the adverb phrase begins with the preposition *for* and ends with the noun *benefit.* Remember that the adverb answers the questions *how? when? where? to what extent?* or *why?*

The adverb phrase does the work of an adverb. It can be used to modify a verb, an adjective, or another adverb. Identify the prepositions and their objects in the sentences above.

EXERCISE A

Identify the adverb phrases in the sentences below.

1. A basket of goodies sat by the door.

2. From the window of the train we saw an old brick schoolhouse.

3. Man shall not live by bread alone.

4. She arrived at London in the morning and stayed for two days.

5. We waited for him for several minutes, but we left in a hurry.

6. The dog jumped over the fence in pursuit of the cat.

7. Wait on the Lord.

8. The youngster confided in his mother about his hopes for a Christmas gift.

9. The track team ran around the track in the pouring rain.

10. From the roof we can see beyond the mountains.

Diagraming

An adverb phrase is diagramed in the same manner as an adjective phrase. It is placed under the word it modifies with the preposition on a slanted line and its object on a horizontal line connected to it.

Example. He ran to the store.

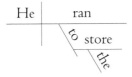

If you have two adjective or adverb phrases modifying the same word, they are connected by a broken line. The conjunction that joins them is written on the broken line.

Example. The squirrel ran up the tree and onto the branch.

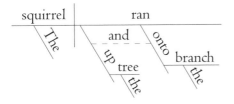

⌛ Historia

The Anglo-Saxon society consisted of small clans or communities, called the *cynn*, and each had its lord. In fact, the earliest word for England, before *Engleland*, was *Angelcynn*. The Anglo-Saxon word for king is *cyn-ing*. The word for lord is *hlaford*, which comes from *hlaf-weard*, meaning the protector of the loaf (loaf is *hlaf*), or the one who provides the bread. The community gathered together to feast in the mead hall, and the lord was seen as both provider and protector, responsible to care for his people. The *wraecca* (wretch) was an exile or wanderer, with no lord and no *cynn*, no community, no fellowship. Anglo-Saxon poetry often deals with the theme of the *wraecca* searching for a new lord, a new community to join. Old English poetry was oral and the poet was called the *scop*. The lord at the feast would call upon the *scop* to sing or recite poetry for the *cynn*. He was an important member of the *cynn*, a public figure, for he recorded and preserved the history and traditions of the *cynn* through his poetry.

Old English poetry is characterized by the *kenning*, a compound descriptive word. Examples include *morning-light* for dawn, *sea-traveler* for ship, *wave-path* or *swan's-riding* for sea, *world-candle* for sun.

(Source: *The Earliest English Poems* by Michael Alexander, Penguin Books, 1966.)

EXERCISE B

Diagram the following sentences, placing adjective and adverb phrases correctly beneath the words they modify.

1. The streets in Moscow are covered with snow.
2. A toddler with his mother's purse wandered out the door and into the yard.
3. In early spring many tulips bloom in the park on the campus.
4. They shopped at the mall for several hours.
5. Thousands of stars appeared in the sky.

LESSON 20

THE PREDICATE MODIFIED BY AN ADVERB CLAUSE

Examples

1. She looked *as if she needed a rest.*
   As if she needed a rest tells *how* she looked.
2. The boy put the stick *where he thought no one would find it.*
   Where he thought no one would find it tells *where* he put it.
3. *Before we leave,* (you) cancel our mail.
   Before we leave tells *when* to cancel the mail. The subject *you* is understood.
4. *Because the weather was wet,* the party was moved indoors.
   Because the weather was wet tells *why* (or *under what condition*) the party was moved.

Explanation

Remember that a subordinate clause is a group of words that has a verb and its subject but cannot stand alone. If the subordinate clause is used to modify a verb, it is an **adverb clause**. An adverb clause will answer *how? where? when? under what condition?* or *why?* Of course an adverb clause can also be used in any way that an adverb can be used: to modify a verb, adjective, or another adverb.

An adverb clause will always begin with a subordinating conjunction. Remember that conjunctions are joining words. The function of the subordinating conjunction is simply to join the adverb clause to the word it is modifying. It has no other grammatical function in the sentence. Memorize the list of subordinating conjunctions so you can easily identify adverb clauses.

> ■ *Definitions*
> An *adverb clause* is a subordinate clause that is used as a single adverb. A *subordinating conjunction* joins an adverb clause to the word it is modifying.

79

Common Subordinating Conjunctions

after	how	until
although	if	when
as	in order that	whenever
as if	lest	where
as long as	since	whereas
as soon as	so that	wherever
as though	than	while
because	that	why
before	though	
but that	unless	

EXERCISE A

In the following sentences identify the adverb clauses and the subordinating conjunction in each clause.

1. Mom sewed on my dress while I watched the little ones.
2. The sky looked as if it might rain any minute.
3. Wherever I walked in the garden, I only saw more splendid sights.
4. Susan brought Sam home so that we could meet him.
5. She set the vase of flowers where we all could see it.
6. When you are ready for us, call us.
7. After she had washed the crystal, she gently set it in the hutch.
8. She polished the silver because it was tarnished quite badly.
9. As soon as he finished his test, he smiled with relief.
10. He ran with the ball as though he were going for a touchdown.

EXERCISE B

Compose three sentences using some of the subordinating conjunctions listed above.

Diagraming

Like the adjective clause, the adverb clause is written below the independent clause on a separate line. The two horizontal lines are joined by a broken line that joins the verb in the adverb clause to the word it is modifying above. The subordinating conjunction is written on the broken line.

▼ *Punctuation Note*

When an adverb clause comes at the beginning of the sentence, it is always followed by a comma. Adverb clauses, when they appear in the middle of the sentence, are enclosed in commas. No comma is needed when it comes at the end of the sentence. (Notice how the sentences in this lesson illustrate the rule.)

Example. Before a test is given, students are warned.

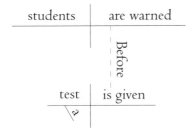

EXERCISE C

Diagram the sentences below.

1. David looks as though he already knew.
2. We will go if the team wins.
3. You should read whenever you can.
4. Unless he arrives soon, the game will be canceled.
5. As soon as you finish, I will begin.

UNIT 2

LESSON 21

THE PREDICATE WITH A DIRECT OBJECT

Examples

1. **He borrowed the *car* for his trip.**
   The subject is *He* and the verb is *borrowed*. He borrowed what? He borrowed the *car*. *Car* is the direct object of the verb *borrowed*.
2. **Our dog bit the *neighbor* on the leg.**
   Our dog bit whom? It bit our *neighbor*.
3. **Susan twisted her *ankle* when she fell.**
   Susan twisted what? She twisted her *ankle*.
4. **Greg dribbled the *ball* past the guard.**
   Greg dribbled what? He dribbled the *ball*.

Explanation

Sometimes the subject and the verb cannot complete the meaning of the sentence. These sentences require a **complement** to complete the meaning. One type of complement is the **direct object**. The direct object directly receives the action or shows the result of the action of the verb. The direct object always answers the questions *whom?* or *what?* of the verb and will always be a noun or a pronoun.

A **transitive verb** can complete the action with the help of an object. *Transitive* means *passing over*. The verb passes over to its object. Verbs that cannot take an object are called **intransitive verbs**. Sometimes the same word can be used as a transitive verb in one sentence and an intransitive verb in another sentence.
Examples.
   She has moved away. (Intransitive)
   I moved the desk. (Transitive)

Exercise A

Find the direct objects in the sentences below. Be sure to ask *whom?* or *what?* after the verb to find the direct object.

1. Ben kicked the ball across the field for a goal.
2. You hit the nail on the head!
3. He pushed the sofa to the den.
4. She lost her purse.
5. Mom wrote a check for their trip.
6. He's reading *A Tale of Two Cities* for literature class.
7. She bought six new trees for the yard.
8. The band played several songs from the forties.
9. I could not read the sign in the dark.
10. He loaded the luggage into the trunk of the car.

Diagraming

To diagram the direct object, simply extend the horizontal line and place the direct object to the right of the verb. A vertical line is drawn to separate the verb from the direct object. This line stops at the base line and does not extend beneath it like the line between the subject and the verb.

Example. She loves cats.

In the case of two direct objects (or compound direct objects), the line is split.
Example. She loves dogs and cats.

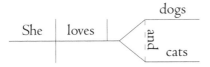

Exercise B

Diagram the sentences below.

1. The church choir sang Christmas carols at the concert.
2. She pasted a stamp on the envelope.

UNIT 2

3. The child licked the lollipop joyously.

4. He opened the letter nervously.

5. We all enjoy football games at outdoor stadiums.

6. She reached the meeting on time.

7. They attended their aunt's funeral in June.

8. The committee sent their findings.

9. The new teacher wrote her name on the board.

10. I heard the birds this morning.

Review Questions

1. What do we call a verb that takes an object?

2. What questions do we ask of the verb to find the direct object?

3. What parts of speech can the direct object be?

LESSON 22

THE PREDICATE WITH AN INDIRECT OBJECT

Examples

1. **The tall woman bent down and gave** *the child* **a handshake.**
   The woman gave what? A *handshake*. To whom? The *child*.
2. **My dad promised** *my mom* **a vacation cruise.**
   My dad promised what? A *cruise*. To whom? My *mom*.
3. **The college sent** *me* **my semester grades.**
   The college sent what? *Grades*. To whom? *Me*.
4. **I gave the** *house* **a fresh coat of paint.**
   I gave what? A *coat* of paint. To what? The *house*.

Explanation

Another type of complement is the **indirect object**. The **indirect object** is a noun or pronoun that is placed between the subject and the direct object and tells *to whom, for whom, to what,* or *for what* the action of the verb is done. A sentence must have a direct object in order to have an indirect object.

EXERCISE A

Identify the indirect and direct objects in the sentences below.

1. The company gave the school a large grant for computers.
2. The instructor handed the students a long reading list.
3. You promised me your cookie recipe.
4. Give Charles my greeting.
5. She sang the baby a lullaby.
6. Mother baked the senior class a cake for their graduation party.
7. My sister made me a velvet dress.

■□ *Definition*

An indirect object is a complement that tells *to/for whom* **or** *to/for what* **the action of the verb is done.**

✒ *N.B.*

Remember, the indirect object will always precede the direct object, and it will never be found in a prepositional phrase.

8. The babysitter read the children a story.
9. I ordered myself a new desk.
10. We poured Mother some tea.

Diagraming

The indirect object is placed beneath the verb on a separate horizontal line. A slanting line connects the indirect object to the main line.

Example. She gave Bob a kiss.

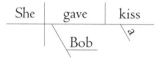

Exercise B

Diagram the sentences below.

1. The baby gave me a smile.
2. Mom sent the college a letter of recommendation.
3. He gave the class a long lecture.
4. My host ordered me a cocktail.
5. The hostess handed me a napkin.

Exercise C

Compose five sentences with direct and indirect objects.

Review Questions

1. Where is the indirect object always located in the sentence?
2. What questions does it answer of the verb?
3. What sort of verb can take an indirect object?

LESSON 23

THE PREDICATE WITH A PREDICATE NOMINATIVE

Examples

1. Jesus is the *way*, the *truth*, and the *light*.

   Jesus is the subject of the sentence. The verb *is* links the subject to the nouns *way*, *truth*, and *light* to identify or explain the subject. *Jesus = way, truth, light*.

2. Yesterday was my *birthday*.

   Yesterday is the subject of the sentence. The verb *was* links the subject to the noun *birthday* to rename or identify the subject. *Yesterday = birthday*.

3. He became a very rich and famous *doctor*.

   He is the subject of the sentence. The verb *became* links the subject to the noun *doctor* to rename or identify the subject. *He = doctor*.

Explanation

Another type of complement is the **subject complement**. These are nouns, pronouns, or adjectives that follow a linking verb. (Refer to Lesson 2 to review linking verbs. A linking verb is used to link or bond the subject to another word in the sentence.) When the word that is linked to the subject is a noun or pronoun, it is called the **predicate nominative**. The predicate nominative is on the predicate or verb side of the sentence, and it names, renames, or identifies the subject. (Remember *nomen* is Latin for *name*.) To check and see if a verb is a linking verb, substitute an equal sign (=) or the verb *is* for the linking verb. If the sentence retains its meaning, it is a linking verb.

Examples.

"To be" verbs:

Gold is a *metal*.

Oxygen is a *gas*.

■☐ *Definition*

The *predicate nominative* is a noun or pronoun that follows a linking verb and identifies, renames, or explains the subject.

87

I am your *teacher*.
They were the *culprits*.
Mr. Smith was the *author*.
She has been a *winner*.
Other linking verbs:
Mary became *queen*.
He remained *president*.
The auction proved a *success*.

EXERCISE A

Identify the predicate nominatives in the sentences below.
1. Raphael was an artist.
2. The whale is the largest mammal.
3. Tadpoles become frogs.
4. Faithfulness is a virtue.
5. The church is the bride of Christ.
6. The boy was a dunce.
7. Lewis and Clark were famous explorers.
8. Jeremy is a fine athlete.
9. The moon is not a star.
10. The boy is my nephew.

N.B.

Personal pronouns must always be in the nominative case when used as a predicate nominative. See Lessons 31 and 33 for more about the *case* of nouns and pronouns.

When a personal pronoun is used as a predicate nominative, it must be of the nominative case. Although we will discuss pronoun cases in detail in Lesson 29, for now you must know that the nominative case personal pronouns are *I, you, he, she, it, we,* and *they*. When a pronoun is needed as a predicate nominative, one of these pronouns must be used. (These are the pronouns that can be used as subjects also.)

Examples.

Correct	*Incorrect*
It is I.	It is me.
Jesus said, "I am He."	I am Him.
This is she.	This is her.
Those are they.	Those are them.

EXERCISE B

Complete the sentences by supplying a predicate nominative. Remember, it must be a noun or pronoun.

1. Iron is _____.
2. My mother was _____.
3. She became _____.
4. They were _____.
5. Milton was _____.
6. Her brother remained _____.
7. I am _____.
8. Joe has become _____.
9. Her favorite book is _____.
10. This will be _____.

Exercise C

Identify the predicate nominatives in these sentences.

1. Children are a heritage from the Lord.
2. The fruit of the womb is His reward.
3. Your children are olive plants around your table.
4. Your wife shall be a fruitful vine.
5. My soul is a weaned child within me.
6. The idols of the nations are silver and gold.
7. Their tongues are serpents full of poison.
8. You are my refuge, O Lord.
9. You are my portion in the land of the living.
10. The Lord is the One who gives salvation to kings.

Diagraming

The predicate nominative is placed on the horizontal line to the right of the verb. It is separated from the verb with a line slanting toward the subject. The slanting line stops at the base line. Any modifiers of the predicate nominative will be placed underneath the word they modify.

Example. The boy is my nephew.

Historia

Anglo-Saxon was the language of Britain for seven centuries, so it is not surprising that we still have some words in our modern tongue that have descended from Anglo-Saxon. *Scot* is an Old-English word meaning treasure or payment. We still use the expression "going *scot*-free." *Tid* means time, and the ocean *tides* keep set times. "At the mead" meant at the feast. A wedding feast was called a *brydealo or bride-ale,* and from that we get our word *bridal. Bridegroom* comes from *bryde* and *guma,* which later became *brydegome* and then our *bridegroom.* Old-English has many negative words that begin with an *n.* Modern English has *nay* and *yay,* one and *none, ever* and *never.*

Exercise D

Diagram the following sentences.

1. My favorite herb is rosemary.
2. Susie's brother is an attorney.
3. My favorite sport is basketball.
4. This is our new teacher.
5. That was her best race.

Review Questions

1. What part of speech must the predicate nominative be?
2. What kind of verb is required for the predicate nominative?
3. What is the job of the predicate nominative?
4. What personal pronouns must be used for the predicate nominative?

LESSON 24

THE PREDICATE WITH A PREDICATE ADJECTIVE

Examples

1. **The Lord is** *gracious* **and** *compassionate.*

   Lord is the subject of the sentence. The linking verb *is* (a *to be* verb) connects the subject to the two adjectives, *gracious* and *compassionate*, which describe *Lord.*

2. **We were** *wrong.*

   The subject is *we.* The linking verb *were* (another *to be* verb) connects the subject to the adjective *wrong. Wrong* describes *we.*

3. **Dinner smells** *good!*

   Good is an adjective describing the subject *dinner. Smells* is the linking verb.

4. **You look** *tired.*

   Look is the linking verb which connects the subject *you* to the adjective *tired.*

Explanation

The other kind of subject complement is the **predicate adjective.** When the word following the linking verb is an adjective describing the subject, it is called a **predicate adjective.** To run the linking verb test, substitute the word *is* for the linking verb, and the sentence should still make sense. *That pie looks delicious. That pie is delicious.* Remember, complements are never found in a prepositional phrase. **Examples.**

  "To be" verbs:
  > Grass *is* green.
  > The sky *is* cloudy today.
  > She *was* unhappy about the test.
  > They *were* late for class.

■☐ *Definition*

A *predicate adjective* is an adjective that follows a linking verb which describes the subject of the sentence.

91

The boys *are* funny.

I *have been* wrong before.

Sense verbs:

She *feels* sorry.

That *sounds* lovely.

The cake *tastes* delicious.

The lake *looks* inviting.

The fresh bread *smells* good.

Other linking verbs:

This painting *appears* quite old.

The lawn *became* dry and brown.

The sea *grew* calm.

She *remains* quite ill.

He *seems* very capable.

Her hair *turned* gray.

The medicine *proved* unhelpful.

My plans went *sour*.

N.B.

Many make the mistake of saying "I feel badly." Because *feel* in this sentence is a linking verb, it must be followed by an adjective, not an adverb. We should say, *"I feel bad." Bad* is an adjective; *badly* is an adverb. To feel badly is to have a poor sense of touch.

EXERCISE A

Identify the predicate adjectives in the sentences below.

1. He is happy who has the God of Jacob for his help.
2. The Lord is righteous.
3. Lord, my heart is not haughty; my eyes are not lofty.
4. The Lord is good to all.
5. Your tabernacle is lovely, O Lord of Hosts!
6. That fragrance smells sweet.
7. Do not be unwise.
8. He is worthy of the honor.
9. The owl looks wise.
10. The children seemed happy.

EXERCISE B

Supply predicate adjectives to make sentences of the words below.

1. You are being _____.
2. The mountain looks _____.
3. He became _____.
4. The water remained _____.

5. This tastes _____.

6. The band sounds _____.

7. The moon seems _____.

8. We feel _____.

9. His paper looks _____.

10. This smells _____.

Diagraming

The predicate adjective is diagramed in the same manner as the predicate nominative.

Example. The bus was late.

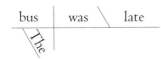

Exercise C

Diagram the sentences below.

1. She was tired and cranky.
2. The field was golden with ripe wheat.
3. The air smells fresh and clean.
4. The young man seemed honest and upright.
5. The puppy was soft and cuddly.
6. This plum tastes terrible.
7. The stars are brilliant tonight.
8. You are wrong.
9. The class was well-behaved today.
10. The snow became slushy quickly.

Review Questions

1. What part of speech will a predicate adjective always be?
2. What kind of verb is required for a predicate adjective?
3. What is the job of the predicate adjective?

LESSON 25

THE NOUN CLAUSE

Examples

1. *Whoever sings in the choir* **must attend the lecture series.**

    The subject of the sentence is *whoever sings in the choir.*

2. **She doesn't remember** *where she put her keys.*

    She doesn't remember *what? Where she put her keys.* The direct object is *where she put her keys.*

3. **The children wave at** *whoever passes by the house.*

    The object of the preposition *at* is *whoever passes by the house.*

4. **His greatest strength is** *that he never gives up.*

    The predicate nominative is *that he never gives up.*

5. **The fact** *that I have no money* **is a real problem.**

    The clause *that I have no money* is acting as an appositive, telling us what the *fact* is.

Explanation

In each of the sentences above, a subordinate clause is taking the place of a noun. In the first sentence a subordinate clause is acting as a **subject**; in the second sentence the clause is a **direct object**; in the third sentence it is the **object of the preposition**; and in the fourth sentence the clause is a **predicate nominative**. In the last sentence the clause is acting as an **appositive** because it is renaming the subject *fact*. These clauses that do the work of nouns are called **noun clauses**.

A **noun clause** is usually introduced by a connective word such as *that*, *whether*, *what*, *who*, *whoever*, *whose*, *where*, or *why*. These words may or may not have any grammatical function in the sentence. In the first and third sentences the introductory word *whoever* is acting as the subject of the clause. In the second sentence *where* is an adverb modifying *put*. In the last two sentences *that* has no grammatical function in the clause.

94

EXERCISE A

Identify the noun clauses in the following sentences and label them as the subject, direct object, object of the preposition, predicate nominative, or appositive in the sentence.

1. I know what you want.
2. The fact that the roof leaks is the reason for the low price.
3. Whether it rains or snows never affects her travel plans.
4. Whoever applies for the job will be considered.
5. The teacher said that our tests were graded.
6. Why you bought tickets to Alaska is beyond me.
7. The lawn will be watered by whoever housesits for us.
8. The reason for the notice is that he hasn't paid his bill.
9. I must write Mother about how she sang.
10. She told me that she had already called you.

EXERCISE B

In the following sentences you will find noun, adjective, and adverb clauses. Find and identify them. Some sentences have more than one subordinate clause.

1. Whenever I travel, I pack only what I absolutely need.
2. No one knows whether he is going to school in the fall.
3. Experienced travelers, who must travel frequently for their jobs, usually know where the best deals are.
4. The flight that we took from San Francisco was very crowded.
5. Because the flight was so long, I felt very groggy when we arrived.
6. The meal that they served wasn't bad.
7. That we made it safely home was my chief desire.
8. I don't know how long I slept.
9. One of the complaints about the food was that it was cold.
10. When the wind blows at our house, the windows shake.

Diagraming

When you diagram a sentence with a noun clause, the noun clause is placed on its own platform and attached to the base line with "stilts." The stilts connect to the base line wherever the noun replaced by the clause would be positioned.

⧗ Historia

Very little is really known about Anglo-Saxon life. But in 1939, when an English farmer discovered a mid-seventh-century Viking ship buried in his field, much new information about our English ancestors was uncovered. The *Sutton Hoo*, a burial ship for a royal person, was found under a mound in East Anglia. The Vikings sometimes buried their great lords in ships, surrounding the dead with their weapons and wealth. Other times they cremated them and built huge mounds over them. Sometimes a ship was buried in honor of a warrior, but the body was put elsewhere. This is the case with the *Sutton Hoo*. Though the body of the warrior was not in the ship, the treasure found included weapons, a shield and helmet, silver spoons, coins, a harp, and other items. This type of burial is recorded in the Anglo-Saxon poem *Beowulf*. The contents of the *Sutton Hoo* can be seen today in the British Museum in London.

Example. Whoever sings in the choir must attend the lecture series.

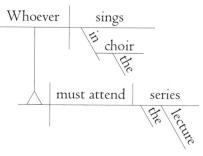

When an introductory word is used with no grammatical connection to the clause, it is placed on a line above the noun clause.

Example. His greatest strength is that he will never quit.

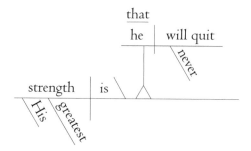

Exercise C

Diagram the following sentences with noun clauses.

1. I heard that you have lost your watch.
2. I know they will do what is right.
3. That they lost the first two games did not discourage them.
4. I bet his plane will be late.
5. The truth is that I am exhausted.
6. I will give you whatever is fair.
7. What his plans are will be a surprise.
8. That some pages are missing is a problem with the book.
9. Invite whomever you want.
10. The buildings will be painted by whomever he hires for the summer.

LESSON 26

SENTENCE STRUCTURE

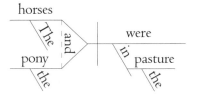

Sentences are classified according to form: they are either **simple**, **compound**, **complex**, or **compound-complex**. We will examine each form below.

The Simple Sentence

The **simple sentence** contains only one subject and one predicate, but either the subject or the verb or both may be compound. A simple sentence consists of one independent clause.

1. The horses were in the pasture.

The subject is *horses*, the predicate is *were in the pasture*.

2. The horses and the pony were in the pasture.

The subject is *horses and the pony*; the predicate is *were in the pasture*.

3. The horses and the pony were spooked and ran away.

The subject is *horses and the pony*; the predicate is *were spooked and ran away*.

In each of the sentences above, *all of the subject* is doing *all of the verb*. A simple sentence consists of one independent clause, but within the one clause there may be several subjects (a compound subject) or more than one verb (a compound verb). In a simple sentence with a compound subject and verb, every verb belongs to every subject, and every subject belongs to every verb.

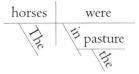
Definition

A *simple sentence* consists of one independent clause.

Diagrams

1. *The horses were in the pasture.*   2. *The horses and the pony were in the pasture.*

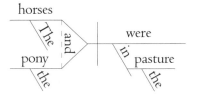

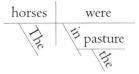

3. *The horses and the pony were spooked and ran away.*

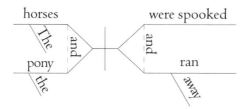

The Compound Sentence

A sentence consisting of two or more independent clauses is called a **compound sentence**. Remember, an independent clause can stand alone, so a compound sentence is the joining of two or more simple sentences into one.

1. **The way was long, the wind was cold, the minstrel was infirm and old.**
    In this sentence three independent clauses are joined together. Though they are closely related, each clause could stand alone.
2. **He called for his pipe, and he called for his bowl, and he called for his fiddlers three.**
    Three independent clauses are joined into one compound sentence.
3. **A cow is a very good animal in the field; but we turn her out of a garden.**
    Again, we see two independent clauses joined into a compound sentence.

Diagrams

The compound sentence is diagramed on two (or more, depending on the number of independent clauses) base lines, with all the modifiers arranged accordingly. The clauses are joined by a dotted line, from verb to verb, with any conjunctions written on the dotted line.

Example. He called for his pipe, and he called for his bowl, and he called for his fiddlers three.

(*Diagram on facing page*)

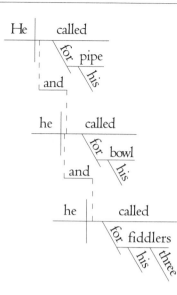

The Complex Sentence

The word *complex* comes from the Latin meaning "woven together." A **complex sentence** is built on a simple sentence: It consists of one independent clause and one or more subordinate (or dependent) clauses. These subordinate clauses may be adverb clauses, adjective clauses, or noun clauses.

1. **When you leave for school today, wear your boots.**

   This complex sentence consists of the adverb clause, *when you leave for school today*, and an independent clause, *wear your boots*.

2. **Because of the heavy snow that fell overnight, school was canceled.**

   The independent clause, *school was canceled*, is modified by the adverb clause, *because of the heavy snow*. The adjective clause, *that fell overnight*, modifies snow.

3. **David Rutherford, who won the speech contest, will speak at the graduation.**

   The noun clause, *who won the speech contest*, is an appositive.

> ■□ *Definition*
> A *complex sentence* consists of one independent clause and one or more subordinate (or dependent) clauses.

The Compound-Complex Sentence

The **compound-complex sentence** is simply a combination of the compound and the complex sentences. It must have at least two independent clauses to make it compound, and it must have at least one subordinate clause to make it complex.

> ■□ *Definition*
> A *compound-complex sentence* is a combination of compound and complex sentences.

⧖ Historia

Sir Robert Cotton (1571-1631) was a collector of ancient manuscripts and old coins, and it is to him that we owe a debt of gratitude for preserving many of the Anglo-Saxon texts that survive today. Most of the works in his library were rescued from monasteries that were being destroyed. His grandson, Sir John Cotton (1621-1701), left the library to England. The library was moved from the Cotton House in 1712 and again relocated in 1730. Unfortunately, a fire on October 23, 1731, destroyed many of the old manuscripts, including the only manuscript of Asser's *Life of King Alfred*. (The destroyed manuscript was probably written around the year 1000.) Thankfully, Archbishop Matthew Parker had printed Asser's work in 1574 and Francis Wise did as well in 1722. So the work is not lost, though there is some debate as to how accurate the printed copies are.

Of the 958 volumes in Cotton's library, 114 were either damaged or destroyed. The remaining books were moved to the British Museum when it was founded in 1753. The Cottonian collection includes the *Lindesfarne Gospels* and other biblical manuscripts, as well as *Beowulf* and *Sir Gawain and the Green Knight*.

1. **When they had crossed over, they came to the land of Gennesaret, and they anchored there.**

   This compound-complex sentence begins with a subordinate adverb clause attached to the first independent clause; the second independent clause is connected with the conjunction *and*.

2. **Wherever He entered, into villages, cities, or the country, they laid the sick in the marketplaces, and they begged Him that they might just touch the border of His garment.**

   The first independent clause has a subordinate adverb clause; the second independent clause has a noun clause.

EXERCISE A

Identify the following sentences as simple (s), compound (cd), complex (cx), or compound-complex (cd-cx).

1. A righteous man who falters before the wicked is like a murky spring and a polluted well (Prov. 25:26).
2. He who gives a right answer kisses the lips (Prov. 24:26).
3. He who covers his sin will not prosper (Prov. 28:13a).
4. Do not forsake your own friend or your father's friend, nor go to your brother's house in the day of your calamity (Prov. 27:10a).
5. Whoever walks blamelessly will be saved, but he who is perverse in his ways will fall at once (Prov. 28:18).

Note: The sentences may seem difficult at first. So, to simplify the process of identification, start by finding any subordinate clauses. Then determine how many independent clauses are in the sentence. This chart may help.

	Independent Clause	Subordinate Clause
Simple	1	
Compound	2 or more	
Complex	1	1 or more
Cd-cx	2 or more	1 or more

Exercise B

Diagram the following sentences.

1. Who can find a virtuous wife?
2. The heart of her husband safely trusts her, so he will have no lack of gain.
3. She seeks wool and flax, and willingly works with her hands.
4. She also rises while it is yet night, and provides food for her household and a portion for her maidservants.
5. Her husband is known in the gates when he sits among the elders of the land.

LESSON 27
REVIEW

Summary

1. A **sentence** is a group of words expressing a complete thought.
2. The **subject** of the sentence is the naming part of the sentence. It represents that part about which something is being said.
3. The subject may be **modified** by the following:
    An **adjective**: *Large* stones rolled down the hillside.
    A **possessive noun**: My *dad's* truck was finally repaired.
    An **appositive**: Milton, *the blind poet*, wrote *Paradise Lost*.
    An **adjective phrase**: The study *of history* is profitable for everyone.
    An **adjective clause**: The old treasure map *that hung on the wall* intrigued the boy.
4. The **predicate** is the preaching part of the sentence or the verb part of the sentence. The predicate does the asserting about the subject.
5. The predicate can be **modified** by the following:
    An **adverb**: The fire burned *brightly*.
    An **adverb phrase**: The smoke drifted *up the chimney*.
    An **adverb clause**: It warmed me *while I studied*.
6. To complete its meaning, some subjects and verbs need a **complement**. There are four kinds of complements. A transitive verb can have a direct and indirect object.
    A **direct object**: The boy kicked the *cat*.
    An **indirect object**: Father sent *Mother* roses on their anniversary.
    An intransitive verb may have a predicate nominative or a predicate adjective.
    A **predicate nominative**: The man is my *father*.
    A **predicate adjective**: The boy grew *tall*.
7. A noun clause can do the work of a noun.
    As a **subject**: *Whoever reaches the barn first* gets the prize.
    Direct object: She learned *that Susie is a poor loser*.

Appositive: The fact *that I am taller* should not bother you.

Predicate nominative: Her only fault is *that she is too generous*.

Object of the preposition: He delivers to *whoever lives in the city limits*.

8. Sentence structure

A **simple sentence** consists of one independent clause.

A **compound sentence** consists of two or more independent clauses.

A **complex sentence** consists of one independent clause and one or more subordinate clauses.

A **compound-complex sentence** consists of two or more independent clauses and at least one subordinate clause.

EXERCISE A: MODIFYING THE SUBJECT

Provide adjectives (or possessive nouns) for the subjects in the following sentences.

1. The swing gently rocked in the wind.
2. My car needs repairs.
3. The clouds covered the mountain.

Reword the sentences above to include adjective phrases modifying the subjects. Write appositives for the subjects in the sentences below.

4. My favorite book lay on the shelf.
5. The boy next door climbs our tree.
6. Susan is an old friend.

Now identify adjective clauses modifying the subjects in the sentences below.

7. The school that I attended has closed.
8. The signed edition of *Tom Sawyer* that my parents found is quite valuable.
9. My brother, who is well-known for his humor, tricked me on April Fools' Day.
10. Our trip to England, which was postponed last year, is approaching soon.

EXERCISE B: MODIFYING THE PREDICATE

Provide an adverb for each verb in the sentences below.

1. The stars are shining.
2. The car skidded.
3. We climbed the mountain.

Now reword the sentences above to include an adverb phrase for each verb in the sentences.

Identify the adverb phrases in the sentences below.

4. The garden was planted in the spring.

5. We harvested during the summer.

6. We took the crops to market.

Identify the adverb clauses in these sentences.

7. Because an ice storm hit last night, stores and offices were closed.

8. I cleaned the house while Mother slept.

9. Since I shopped for Christmas early, I have all my gifts.

10. When you have finished mowing the lawn, please trim the hedge.

Exercise C: Overall Review

In the sentences below identify adjective (adj) and adverb (adv) clauses, noun clauses (n), direct (do) and indirect objects (io), predicate nominatives (pn), and predicate adjectives (pa).

1. The stone which the builders rejected has become the chief cornerstone.

2. I will meditate on Your precepts and contemplate Your ways.

3. I see wondrous things from Your law.

4. I am a stranger in the earth.

5. (You) Give me understanding, and I shall keep Your law.

6. I shall observe it with my whole heart.

7. I hope for Your salvation, and I do Your commandments.

8. My soul keeps Your testimonies, and that I love them exceedingly is true.

9. The entirety of Your word is truth, and every one of Your righteous judgments endures forever.

10. The Lord will be your confidence.

11. His truth shall be your shield and buckler.

12. He is my refuge and my fortress.

13. He is our God, and we are the people of His pasture, and the sheep of His hand.

14. The Lord God is a sun and a shield.

15. The Lord will give grace and glory to whoever cries out to Him.

16. You were once darkness, but now you are light in the Lord.

17. For we are members of His body.

18. That the husband is the head of the wife is taught in Scripture.

19. When sin has conceived, it gives birth to death.

20. If any of you lacks wisdom, ask God.

21. Blessed is the man who endures temptation.

⌛ Historia

In the late ninth century A.D., the Vikings (or Danes) began invading Britain. King Alfred the Great was finally able to stop their advance, and he made peace with them at the Treaty of Wedmore in 878. This treaty made the Danes stay in the northeastern section of England, a region that was called "Danelaw." After Alfred's death in 899, the Danish king Canute brought England under Danish domination. England continued under Danish rule from 1016 to 1042. During the two hundred years that the Danish were present in Britain, they intermingled freely with the English and left their impact on the language. This shows up today mostly in northern England in place names that end with *-by, -beck, -dale, -fell*, etc. If you have an English last name that ends with *-son* or *-sen*, it is probably of Danish origin. The Danish also contributed words like *sky, skin, ugly, anger, low, wrong, husband, gate, die, take*, and *want*. But their influence is probably most strongly felt in our grammar, for they gave us the pronouns *they, them*, and *their*.

22. When he has been proved, he will receive the crown of life which the Lord has promised to those who love Him.

23. When the chief shepherd appears, you will receive the crown of glory that does not fade away.

24. He who has begun a good work in you will complete it until the day of Jesus Christ.

25. This is the disciple who testifies of these things.

26. His hope is that you might believe.

EXERCISE D

Now go back and identify each sentence above as simple (s), compound (cd), complex (cx), or compound-complex (cd-cx).

EXERCISE E

Diagram sentences 8, 9, 16, 19, and 20 from Exercise C above.

UNIT THREE

SPECIAL PROPERTIES OF NOUNS AND PRONOUNS

Nouns and pronouns are not quite so simple as they might first appear. They have many aspects like **gender**, **number**, and **case**. Although nouns are fairly unchanging as they take on different attributes, pronouns are often irregular and have the additional aspect of **person**.

CONTENTS

LESSON 28

TYPES OF NOUNS

Explanation

The two large categories of nouns are proper nouns and common nouns. But common nouns can be classed as concrete, abstract, or collective.

1. **Proper nouns** name particular things and are capitalized: *Doug, Washington, Bible*.
2. **Common nouns** name general classes of things: *street, park, man, book*.

> **Concrete nouns** name physical things that can be seen, touched, or tasted: *tree, plate, car, flower*.
>
> **Abstract nouns** name concepts, qualities, or conditions: *strength, wisdom, beauty*.
>
> **Collective nouns** name collections of objects: *flock, choir, audience, jury, family*.

■☐ *Definitions*

Proper nouns name particular things. *Common* nouns name classes of things. *Concrete* nouns name things in the physical world. *Abstract* nouns name any non-physical thing that we can think of. *Collective* nouns name groups of things.

Examples

1. The *man* is *Mr. Robert Stuart*.

   In this sentence the noun *man* is common and *Mr. Robert Stuart* is a proper noun. *Man* can be classed as a concrete noun.
2. The *students* were discussing a biblical view of *liberty*.

   The noun *students* is also common and concrete. It can be seen or touched. However, the noun *liberty* is abstract. It cannot be touched or tasted.
3. The stray *cow* joined the *herd*.

   The noun *cow* is simply a common, concrete noun, but the noun *herd* is a collective noun, for it names a group or collection of things.

EXERCISE

In the following excerpt from "The Ugly Duckling" by Hans Christian Andersen, identify the common nouns in italics as concrete, abstract, or collective.

In this snug *retreat* sat a *duck* upon her nest, watching for her young *brood* to hatch; but the *pleasure* she had felt at first was almost gone; she had begun to think it a wearisome *task*, for the little ones were so long in coming out of their *shells*, and she seldom had *visitors*. The other ducks liked much better to swim about in the *canals* than to climb the slippery banks, and sit under the burdock leaves to have a *gossip* with her. It was a long *time* to stay so much by herself.

LESSON 29

NUMBER: SINGULAR AND PLURAL

Nouns have **number**. They may be *singular* (book) or *plural* (books). Several rules govern the formation of the plural. English is not a tidy language on this point. Though you can memorize the rules below, if you are unsure of the plural form, consult the dictionary.

1. Generally the plural is formed by adding *s* or *es* to the singular form of the noun.
   a. If the final sound will unite easily to the sound of *s*, the plural is formed by simply adding *s*. Examples: *tree, trees; cat, cats; boat, boats.*
   b. If the final sound of the word will not easily unite with the *s* sound, an *es* is added. This is true of words ending in *s, x, z, sh,* and *ch.* Examples: *fox, foxes; lash, lashes; waltz, waltzes; glass, glasses; bench, benches.*

2. If the word ends in a silent *e*, an *s* is added. Examples: *rose, roses; voice, voices.*

3. Most nouns that end in *o* and are preceded by a consonant form their plural by adding *es*. Examples: *hero, heroes; cargo, cargoes.* Exceptions: *patio, memento, zero, two.* Other exceptions include words related to music: *solo, solos; piano, pianos; soprano, sopranos; alto, altos; quarto, quartos; octavo, octavos; canto, cantos.*

4. Some nouns ending in *f* or *fe* form their plural by changing the *f* to a *v* and adding *es*. Examples: *knife, knives; loaf, loaves; life, lives; shelf, shelves; wolf, wolves; thief, thieves.*

5. Other nouns ending in *f* or *fe* just add *s* to form the plural. Examples: *chief, chiefs; belief, beliefs; cliff, cliffs; surf, surfs; gulf, gulfs.*

6. Nouns that end in *y* after a consonant form the plural by changing the *y* to an *i* and adding *es*. Examples: *lady, ladies; spy, spies; enemy, enemies; glory, glories.*

7. Nouns that end in *y* after a vowel form the plural regularly, by adding *s*. Examples: *day, days; turkey, turkeys.*

8. Some nouns form their plural in irregular ways. Examples: *man, men; child, children; woman, women; tooth, teeth; foot, feet; ox, oxen.*

UNIT 3

■❑ *Definition*

The *number* of a noun refers to how many things the noun names. If it names one thing, the number is *singular*. If it names more than one thing, it is *plural*.

 *Punctuation Note*

When you are referring to a word as a word, or a letter as a letter, you must write it in italics. Plurals of words and letters in italics are formed by adding an apostrophe and -*s* in normal type. For example, "I rewrote my paper, deleting all the *there*'s." Another example: "I don't like the *f*'s in this font."

   When referring to time periods with year numbers, just an -*s* is added (no apostrophe), as in "the 1990s."

⧖ Historia

The aggressive Vikings were a terror to the English. They attacked suddenly and savagely from the sea in their ships. The monastery at Lindisfarne is one example of their brutal assaults. Lindisfarne was founded as a mission outreach to the English in 635 by Aidan, an Irish monk, and it later became a well-known center of learning. Aidan was succeeded as the abbot of the monastery by a monk named Eadfrith, who is famous for producing the *Lindisfarne Gospels*. Completed in 698, the *Lindisfarne Gospels* are extraordinary illuminated texts of the gospels written in Latin on calf-skin parchment called *vellum*. The opening words of each gospel are decorated with elaborate designs. A hundred years later, in 793, the Vikings unexpectedly appeared at Lindisfarne, slaughtering the monks and destroying the church there. *The Anglo-Saxon Chronicle* reads: "On the sixth of the Ides of June the ravaging of the heathen men lamentably destroyed God's church at Lindisfarne." The raids are recorded again in 801 and 806. In 867 the rebuilt abbey was burned. By 875 the surviving monks moved to a safer spot, taking the body of King Ceolwulf with them. King Ceolwulf had been king of the Northumbrians from 729-737, but gave up his crown to enter the monastery at Lindisfarne. In the twelfth century a priory church was constructed on the site of the seventh-century Anglo-Saxon church that had been destroyed. The ruins of the priory church can be seen today.

9. Compound nouns (that include modifiers) usually form their plural by making the noun plural. Examples: *daughter-in-law, daughters-in-law; runner-up, runners-up*.

10. Some compound nouns form their plural in other ways. Examples: *three-year-old, three-year-olds; drive-in, drive-ins*.

11. Some nouns are the same in the singular and plural form. Examples: *deer, trout, salmon, sheep, series, species, mathematics*.

12. Foreign words form the plural either in the same way as the original language or in the English way of adding *s* or *es*. Examples: *alumnus, alumni; parenthesis, parentheses; formula, formulas; index, indexes*.

13. Letters, numbers, and signs form the plural by adding an apostrophe and *s*. Words considered as words form their plural the same way. Examples: twelve *a*'s; three *3*'s; several *also*'s.

EXERCISE

Form the plural of the following nouns.

1. bush, roof, hero, thief
2. man, child, ox, lady
3. drive-in, salmon, sheep, glass
4. ship, soprano, chief, penny
5. potato, son-in-law, cruise, wife

LESSON 30

GENDER

Nouns express one of four **genders** in English.

1. When the noun refers to the male, it is **masculine**: *bull, rooster, stallion, bridegroom, priest.*
2. When the noun refers to the female, it is **feminine**: *sister, nun, bride, duchess, heroine, hostess.*
3. When the noun can refer to either male or female it is **common**: *student, citizen, voter, teacher, driver.*
4. And when the noun has no reference to either sex, it is **neuter**: *window, hillside, cloud, wind, rain, log, root.* The word *neuter* is from Latin meaning "neither." Therefore, neuter is neither masculine nor feminine.

The feminine and masculine gender are formed three different ways:

1. By using completely different words, as in *sister, brother; husband, wife.*
2. By changing the ending of the word, as in *actor* and *actress; lion* and *lioness.*
3. By using a prefix, as in *she-goat, he-goat,* and *male-child.*

EXERCISE A

Identify the gender of each of the nouns listed below.

1. Bell, uncle, strawberry, girl, neighbor, sister, tree, rose, grass.
2. Truth, goodness, clock, children, grandmother, soldier, people, statesman.
3. Stag, landlady, heir, tiger, giant, countess, train, brook.
4. Son, mare, lad, hero, czar, client, conductor, tailor, princess, book.

REVIEW QUESTIONS

1. Name the five categories of nouns.
2. What does it mean for a noun to have number?

N.B.

Though English has no fixed rule to determine which inanimate nouns are masculine and which are feminine, traditionally, abstract nouns, ships, cities, and countries are usually considered feminine.

UNIT 3

3. What are the four genders a noun can have?

4. How is the plural formed in a word that ends in a silent *e*?

5. How is the plural formed when the word ends in *ch*, *sh*, *z*, *x*, or *s*?

6. If a word ends in *y* after a consonant, how is the plural formed?

7. How is the plural formed of the word *mother-in-law*?

8. What rule governs many words related to music?

9. How do we form the plural of numbers, letters, or signs?

10. What must we do with words referred to as words?

LESSON 31

CASE: NOMINATIVE, OBJECTIVE, AND POSSESSIVE

Nouns and pronouns are always related in some way to other words in the sentence. Nouns can be used many different ways: as a subject, predicate nominative, direct object, indirect object, possessive, appositive, or an object of a preposition.

In Latin and Greek, as well as in Old English, the usage of the noun is shown by a special form called **case.** Case denotes the relationship of the noun to other words in the sentence. Though Old English showed case by different forms of the nouns, this fell into disuse after the Norman Conquest. Modern English has only one survivor of the old forms, and that is the *'s* added to show possession. Now the relation of the noun to other parts of the sentence is shown by its position in the sentence. English has three cases: **nominative, objective**, and **possessive.**

1. A noun is in the **nominative** case when it is used as the *subject* or *predicate nominative.*
2. A noun is in the **objective** case when it is used as a *direct object, indirect object,* or *object of a preposition.*
3. A noun is in the **possessive** case when it is used to show possession (*Peter's map*).

In English the noun form does not change if it is in the nominative or objective case. *The cat ate the fish. The fish ate the cat.* In both examples the nouns are in the same form even though they are used differently in the sentence. However, nouns are inflected in their plural forms (for example, by adding *s*) and in their possessive forms (by adding an apostrophe and an *s*). Unlike the noun, the pronoun (as you will see in Lesson 33) changes significantly when it changes case.

■☐ *Definition*

The *case* of a noun refers to how the noun is used in the sentence.

⧗ *Historia*

In 893 a Welsh monk in King Alfred's service named Asser wrote (in Latin) the *Life of King Alfred,* which is the earliest known biography of an Anglo-Saxon king. Though little is known of Asser, he was one of the men who helped King Alfred in translating selected important works from Latin to Anglo-Saxon. Because the Vikings had ransacked and destroyed many of the libraries in the monasteries, Alfred undertook the important task of restocking the libraries with copies of important works. Alfred was hungry for learning and had most likely learned Latin from his own advisors who read aloud to him from Latin works. Asser says, "One day when we were sitting together in the royal chamber discussing all sorts of topics (as we normally did), it happened that I was reading aloud some passage to him from a certain book. As he was listening intently to this with both ears and carefully mulling it over in the depths of his mind, he suddenly showed me a little book which he constantly carried on his person, and in which were written … some psalms and certain prayers which he had learned in his youth. He told me to copy the passage in question into the little book" (Asser, chapter 88).

Nominative Case

Remember that the word *nominative* is related to the Latin *nomen* which means *name.* The nominative case is used for the subject of the sentence or the predicate nominative. Because English does not have case endings for nouns (except the possessive case), we have no endings to memorize.

Example. *The rain continued for the afternoon. Rain* is in the nominative case because it is the subject.

Objective Case

The objective case is used for all objects. This includes the direct object, indirect object, and object of the preposition. If you have studied Latin, you are familiar with the dative case (which is used for the indirect object) and the accusative case (which is used for the direct object); these are merged in English to be the objective case.

Examples. *I love the rain. Rain* is the direct object. *God gave the land more rain. Land* is the indirect object; *rain* is the direct object. *She prayed for rain. Rain* is the object of the preposition. In all these sentences, *rain* is in the objective case.

Possessive Case

The possessive case simply shows ownership. Nouns in the possessive case must use an apostrophe and *s* to show possession.

Examples. *My uncle's antiques are in splendid shape. The boy's shoes were falling off his feet. My, uncle's, his,* and *boy's* are all in the possessive case; the nouns have the added apostrophe and *s.* The pronoun possessives will be discussed in Lesson 33.

EXERCISE A

Name the case of the italicized nouns in the following sentences. Be able to explain your answer.

1. *Susan* returned the *volleyballs* to the *teacher.*
2. The *speaker* delivered the *address* about *femininity* to a large *audience.*
3. *Lewis* and *Clark* were famous *explorers* in the *Northwest.*
4. This is the finest *restaurant* in the *area.*
5. The *horse's owner* was worried about the *race.*

EXERCISE B

Now identify the number and gender of each italicized noun below.

1. *Susan* returned the *volleyballs* to the *teacher*.
2. The *speaker* delivered the *address* about *femininity* to a large *audience*.
3. *Lewis* and *Clark* were famous *explorers* in the *Northwest*.
4. This is the finest *restaurant* in the *area*.
5. The *horse's owner* was worried about the *race*.

LESSON 32

THE DECLENSION OF A NOUN

◼☐ *Definition*
The *declension* of a noun is an ordered presentation of all the forms the noun can take, organized by number and case.

When we arrange the inflection of nouns or pronouns in order, according to their case and number, it is called **declension**. To decline a noun is to express all its cases and numbers in a systematic way. Look at the example below of the declension of *father* and *man*.

Case	Singular	Plural	Singular	Plural
Nominative	father	fathers	man	men
Objective	father	fathers	man	men
Possessive	father's	fathers'	man's	men's

Unlike Latin and Greek, our English nouns have the same form in both the nominative and objective cases. *Man* is the same whether it is used as the subject (nominative case) or as the object (objective case). We only see a difference in the possessive form. We might think we could dispense with the two cases and simply have one. However, our pronouns still have distinct forms in the nominative and objective cases (he, him; she, her; they, them). This we will see in the next lesson.

EXERCISE A
Decline the following nouns. Arrange in the same order as above: nominative (singular, plural), objective (singular, plural), possessive (singular, plural).
1. child
2. beauty
3. tongue
4. soil
5. family

Review Exercise

For each of the italicized nouns in the sentences below, name the type of noun, its number, gender, case, and usage.

Example (from sentence 1). *Settlement:* common, singular, neuter, nominative, subject.

1. The oldest *settlement* in our country is *St. Augustine*, Florida.
2. It was founded by the *Spanish* in 1595.
3. The *Frenchman* Champlain planted a *colony* in *Canada* forty *years* later where Quebec now stands.
4. While on an *expedition* in New York *state*, *Champlain* discovered the *lake* that bears his *name*.

THE PERSONAL PRONOUN: GENDER, PERSON, NUMBER, AND CASE

Explanation

Pronouns, like nouns, have **number** and **gender** as well as **case**. They also reflect **person**. Before we proceed to case, let's examine the gender, person, and number of pronouns.

I. Gender

Pronouns that reflect the **masculine**: *he, him, his*

Pronouns that reflect the **feminine**: *she, her, hers*

Pronouns that are **common**: *they, them, theirs, their*

Pronouns that are **neuter**: *it, its*

2. Person

First person is the person speaking: *I, we, me, us*

Second person is the person spoken to: *you, thee, thou*

Third person is the person spoken of: *he, she, it, they, him, her, them*

3. Number

Singular includes *I, you, he, she, it, me, him, her*

Plural includes *we, you, they, us, them*

4. Case: Nominative, Objective, and Possessive

Nominative Case

	Singular	Plural
First person:	*I*	*we*
Second person:	*you*	*you*
Third person:	*he, she, it*	*they*

Pronouns in the nominative case must be used as the subject or as the predicate nominative.

Subject:

I am going fishing.

He is my father-in-law.

They will win the prize.

She and *I* are good friends.

Predicate nominative:

That is *she*.

The winner will be *he*.

Those people are *they*.

It is *we* who should be going.

In an incomplete construction after the word *than* or *as*, it is sometimes difficult to determine the correct pronoun. For example, *He is taller than* _____ (*I* or *me*). It will help you select the correct pronoun if you finish the statement: *He is taller than I am.* Another example: *She is as old as* _____ (*I* or *me*). *She is as old as I am.* In the following examples of incomplete construction, the choice of pronoun is important to the meaning of the sentence.

1. I like Sue better than *he*. I like Sue better than *he does*, or I like Sue better than *he likes Sue*.

2. I like Sue better than *him*. I like Sue better than *I like him*.

The choice of pronoun makes a significant change in the meaning of the sentence.

Oral Exercise

Read the following sentences aloud. Each is using nominative case pronouns.

1. He and Robert are old friends.

2. Debbie and she plan to travel to London this summer.

3. Either Dad or he will book the tickets.

4. Neither Sue nor he is going to the airport.

5. We teachers must read all the applications.

6. When will you and she come for lunch?

7. The musicians and we vocalists must be on stage early.

8. After much coaxing, he and she became friends again.

9. Are she and I roommates this year?

10. My grandparents and they are taking us to Europe.

Objective Case

	Singular	Plural
First person:	*me*	*us*
Second person:	*you*	*you*
Third person:	*him, her, it*	*them*

Pronouns used as objects must be in the objective case.

Direct object:

Mary called *me*.

The child kicked *her*.

We picked up Sue and *him*.

Indirect object:

The owner gave *him* the job.

The company sent *me* a replacement.

Object of the preposition:

The dog ran over to *us*.

My parents bought it from *them*.

A common pronoun error is using the wrong case when a compound subject or object is used. For example: *She gave Bill and me a ride to work.* *Bill* and *me* are both indirect objects, thus the objective case pronoun must be used. If you are unsure, delete the first object: *She gave me a ride to work.* Your ear tells you that *She gave I a ride to work* is incorrect. This principle is the same with a compound subject as well. *Ben and he rode their bikes to the park*, not *Ben and him rode their bikes to the park*. When a pronoun is used with an appositive, use the same case as would be required without the appositive.

Examples.

We mothers are very busy.

We are very busy.

Possessive Case

	Singular	Plural
First person:	*my, mine*	*our, ours*
Second person:	*your, yours*	*your, yours*
Third person:	*his, her, hers, its*	*their, theirs*

Possessive case is used as a possessive adjective, modifying a noun to show possession. It is also used as a predicate adjective, modifying the subject. Remember that possessive pronouns do not require apostrophes.

Possessive adjective:

That is *my* sister.
Where is *your* hat?
Fred is *his* best friend.
This is *our* home.
Their cat had kittens.

Predicate adjective:

The prize is *mine*.
This gift is *yours*.
The car is *hers*.
The work is *theirs*.

Exercise A

Select the correct pronouns in the following sentences.

1. She knew it was (I, me).
2. She and (he, him) will go together.
3. May Liz and (I, me) leave now?
4. Mom expects you and (I, me) for dinner.
5. It was either (she, her) or her mother who answered the phone.
6. When will you and (they, them) come again?
7. Have you seen Mark and (he, him) together?
8. Not many could sing as well as (she, her).
9. This is the new mind-set among (we, us) Americans.
10. Scott can run faster than (he, him).

Exercise B

Identify the person and number of the italicized pronouns in the following sentences. Then go back and identify gender and case of the same pronouns.

1. *She* gives much time and money to *her* favorite charities.
2. The boys ran through *their* backyard to *my* house.
3. *He* received a letter from *his* uncle.
4. Mother gave *them* a much deserved spanking in *her* bedroom.
5. *They* will meet *us* at *our* boat dock.

6. *It* is *they* at the door now.
7. If *he* bothers *you* again, let *me* know.
8. Give *him* *my* regards.
9. David and *he* are regulars at the cafe.
10. The winners are Susan and *she*.

LESSON 34

WHO, WHOM, AND WHOSE

Now that you understand *case*, it should be easy to determine when to use *who* and when to use *whom*. This pronoun is *inflected*, meaning that the ending of the word changes depending on how it is used. *Who* is in the nominative case, so it must be used as the subject or predicate nominative. Example: *Who is that young man? Whom* is the objective case and must be used as an object. Example: *She is the girl of whom we speak. Whose*, of course, shows possession and is used as an adjective (some refer to it as a pronoun adjective, or pronominal adjective). Example: *Whose book is this?*

Who or Whom?

When *who* or *whom* is used as a relative pronoun in an adjective clause, it is especially important to determine the function of the word in the sentence before determining which form to use. Because the relative pronoun has a grammatical function within the clause (and is not simply used to join the adjective clause to the independent clause), you must first determine whether it is being used as a subject or as an object. Consider the examples below.

1. *Who is coming to dinner?* The subject of the sentence is *who*. Nominative case.
2. *He is the guest whom they invited this morning.* The adjective clause is *whom they invited this morning.* The subject of the clause is *they. They invited whom this morning. Whom* is a direct object, so it must be in the objective case.
3. *The winner is who?* Rearrange the sentence to make a statement: *Who is the winner.* The subject is *who*.
4. *Ben is the student who won the scholarship. Who won the scholarship* is the adjective clause. *Who* is the subject of the clause, so it is nominative case.
5. *You gave the report to whom? Whom* is the object of the preposition.

⌛ Historia

The *Battle of Maldon* is another Anglo-Saxon poem or song that was composed to commemorate a battle against the Viking invaders in 991. Its 325 verses demonstrate, like *Beowulf,* the heroic ethic of loyalty to one's lord. Most of the song is about Byrhtnoth and the loyal English Christians who fought for him. The original manuscript from the eleventh century was in the same manuscript that contained Asser's *Life of King Alfred* that was destroyed in the fire in the Cotton library in 1731. Thankfully, a copy of the poem had been made by one of the library staff, and that is all that is available today. However, before the copy was made, the beginning and the end of the poem had been lost. The copy that is preserved today begins "....would be broken." Byrhtnoth was an *ealdorman.* This word initially meant ruler or warrior, but in later Old English it meant a member of the land-holding aristocracy. In both cases it was a title that was second only to king. Byrhtnoth is described as white-haired, implying he was probably sixty-five years old or more at the time of the battle. A twelfth-century historian describes Byrhtnoth as "eloquent, robust, of great bodily stature...remarkably brave and free from the fear of death." A letter from 1772 describes an investigation into Byrhtnoth's tomb and estimates he was about six foot nine. The poem records for us the details of the battle. The

Continued on next page

EXERCISE A

In the sentences below, first find the adjective clause. Then decide how the relative pronoun is used in the clause. Next select the correct form of the pronoun.

1. That is the woman (who, whom) we voted for. (*Hint*: That is the woman for [who, whom] we voted.)
2. That is the man (who, whom) responded to my ad.
3. Do you know (who, whom) I am?
4. My father is a person (who, whom) we all greatly admire.
5. Do you know (who, whom) the city is named after?
6. Famous American poets were among the writers (who, whom) we studied.

EXERCISE B

Fill in the blank with *who* or *whom*.

1. _____ do you mean?
2. _____ have we here?
3. _____ will you invite?
4. _____ did you give it to?
5. _____ do you think I am?
6. _____ are you writing to?
7. _____ were you talking to?
8. _____ did she call?
9. I don't know _____ to send.
10. _____ was speaking to you?
11. I do not know _____ he has met.
12. _____ did you say sat beside you?
13. _____ do you think will be elected?
14. _____ should I meet yesterday but my old friend Jones!
15. _____ do you think called?
16. _____ do you know in your class?
17. You called _____ at the office?
18. Give the invitations to (whoever, whomever) you wish.
19. _____ is that woman?
20. He is going to be married to _____?

Whose

Whose is a relative pronoun used to modify a noun. It can also be used to join an adjective clause to another clause. When *whose* begins an adjective clause, it will still be modifying a word in the clause. *Whose* is in the possessive case.

Examples.

Whose book is this? Whose is modifying the subject as a predicate adjective. (*This book is whose?*)

The man apologized to the woman whose car he had dented. The adjective clause modifying woman is *whose car he had dented.* The subject of the clause is *he.* The verb is *had dented. Car* is the direct object, and *whose* is modifying car.

EXERCISE C

Here's a challenge. Diagram the last sentence used as an example above: *The man apologized to the woman whose car he had dented.* Remember, the adjective clause goes on a separate line beneath the independent clause.

Continued from previous page

Vikings would have been easily destroyed, except Byrhtnoth let them land safely so they could fight more fairly. The elderly Byrhtnoth led the charge against the heathen Vikings, but he was cut down. Though many of his followers fled, a few of the faithful remained and fought to the end.

UNIT 3

LESSON 35

OTHER PRONOUNS

We have already studied *personal pronouns* and *relative pronouns* that introduce adjective and noun clauses. Here we will discuss *interrogative, demonstrative, indefinite,* and *reflexive* pronouns.

Interrogative Pronouns

■□ Definitions

Interrogative pronouns are used to ask about someone or something of unknown identity. They are who, whom, whose, which, and what.

   Demonstrative pronouns, on the other hand, point out specific persons or things. They are this, these, that, and those.

Interrogative pronouns are used to ask questions. They include *who, whom, whose, which,* and *what.* When *which* or *what* or *whose* is followed by a noun, it is a pronoun adjective (or pronominal adjective) because it is doing the work of an adjective. *Whose book* is it? *Which page* are you reading? *What name* have you selected? *Whose* can be used as a predicate adjective, as in *The book is whose?* Otherwise, interrogative pronouns do the work of pronouns, taking the place of nouns. They can do anything that a noun can do.

    Subject of the sentence: *Who* is leaving?
    Direct Object: *Whom* do you love? *Which* do you want? *What* do you want?
    Indirect Object: You gave *whom* a kiss?
    Object of the Preposition: You gave the bill to *whom?*
    Predicate Nominative: *What* is his name? (His name is *what?*)

Demonstrative Pronouns

Demonstrative pronouns are used to point out specific things or specific persons. They include *this* and its plural *these,* and *that* and its plural *those. This* and *these* refer to things that are near in time, space, or thought; *that* and *those* refer to things that are farther away.

    1. The demonstrative pronouns can take the place of nouns.
        These are my parents. *This* is my home. *That* is my brother.
    2. The demonstrative pronouns may be used as pronominal adjectives.

These roads need repairs. *This* sign points the way. *That* boy is my brother. *Those* shoes are dusty.

Indefinite Pronouns

Indefinite pronouns do not refer to specific persons or things. They make a rather lengthy list:

All, another, any, anybody, anyone, anything, both, each, each other, either, everybody, everyone, everything, few, many, more, most, much, neither, nobody, none, no one, one, one another, other, several, some, somebody, someone, such.

Indefinite Pronouns may refer to the following:

1. Individuals of a class taken separately: *each, neither, either.*
2. Words dealing with number or quantity: *all, any, both, few, many, much, several, some, one, none.*
3. Phrasal pronouns: *each other, one another.*

Indefinite pronouns can take the place of nouns as in the following examples:

All were present.
Both ordered the special.
Few attended the meeting.
Several wrote letters.

Of course, these pronouns can also be used as pronominal adjectives:

Each boy answered in turn.
Several ducks flew from the pond.
Some clouds gathered overhead.

 Definition
Indefinite pronouns are used to refer to classes or various numbers of persons or things, but not any one in particular.

Reflexive Pronouns

A reflexive pronoun refers back to the subject of the verb. They are used either for emphasis or after a verb or preposition to refer back to the subject. Reflexive pronouns are compound personal pronouns that are formed by adding the suffix *-self* or *-selves: myself, yourself, himself, herself, itself, ourselves, yourselves, themselves.*

1. Reflexive pronouns are used for emphasis.

I *myself* have seen it.
I will do it *myself.*
We saw the man *himself.*
The mountains *themselves* tremble in the presence of God.

2. They are also used as direct objects, indirect objects, or objects of the preposition.

Definition
Reflexive pronouns take the place of the subject of the sentence or clause.

UNIT 3

He thinks too much of *himself.*

Love thy neighbor as *thyself.*

Don't be so hard on *yourself.*

I cut *myself.*

He saw *himself* in the mirror.

We gave *ourselves* a day off.

Give *yourself* plenty of time to finish.

The reflexive pronouns should not be used to replace the simple personal pronouns. For example, *She invited Mary and myself to dinner.* The sentence should be *She invited Mary and me to dinner.*

EXERCISE A

Identify all the pronouns in italics as interrogative (it), demonstrative (d), indefinite (id), or reflexive (r).

1. *Whose* is that?
2. *These* are my mother's pearls.
3. *This* is my old favorite. *Which* is yours?
4. *Who* do you think she is?
5. *What* does that sign say?
6. *Each* said his prayers.
7. She said she would do it *herself.*
8. *Nobody* could agree on a date.
9. *Several* showed up late.
10. *Which* would you like?

PRONOUN AGREEMENT

Examples

1. **Each boy brought** *his* **own bat and ball to the game.**

   The singular pronoun *his* refers to the singular noun *boy*. The masculine pronoun *his* is used because the antecedent *boy* is masculine.

2. **The boys brought** *their* **fathers to the game.**

   The plural pronoun *their* refers to the plural noun *boys*. The common pronoun *their* can be used with either a feminine or masculine noun.

3. **The woman cared for** *her* **sick baby at home.**

   The singular, feminine pronoun *her* refers to the singular, feminine noun *woman*.

4. **She dropped the ticket, and the man picked** *it* **up.**

   The singular, neuter noun *ticket* is replaced by the singular, neuter pronoun *it*.

Explanation

The pronoun must always agree in number and gender with its antecedent. Remember the *antecedent* is the word the pronoun replaces or stands for. (Refer to Lesson 5.) If the antecedent is singular, the pronoun should be singular; if the antecedent is plural, the pronoun must be plural. In the same way, if the noun is neuter, the pronoun used should be neuter. If the noun refers to either masculine or feminine, a common pronoun is used.

Examples.

   On the seventh day, God ended *His* work.

   Every tree is known by *its* fruit.

The following rules explain correct pronoun usage.

■☐ *Definition*
Agreement between a pronoun and its antecedent means that they have the same number and gender.

Rule 1: The following pronouns are regarded as singular, and when they are used as antecedents, they require singular pronouns. Notice that all the pronouns that end with -one or -body are **singular**: *each, every, either, neither, one, everyone, everybody, no one, nobody, any, anyone, anybody, someone, somebody.* The pronouns used to refer to these are **singular**. Notice in each of the sentences below the use of the singular pronoun to refer to the antecedent.

1. Each of the sisters has *her* [not *their*] own room.
2. Either Sue or Karen will bring *her* car.
3. Neither boy can spell *his* own name.
4. Everyone must mind *his* manners.
5. Nobody brought *his* sheet music to choir practice.
6. Everybody gave according to *his* ability.
7. Someone left *his* book.

When referring to a person or persons generally (when the antecedent is common—either feminine or masculine), it is standard to use the masculine pronoun. This is not a slight to women in any way. It is simply a generic reference to people. Though it has become common today to alternate the pronoun (using first the masculine and then the feminine so as not to give undue offense), this is an unnecessary distraction. Note examples 4, 5, 6, and 7 above. Similarly, if the antecedents are both male and female, the masculine pronoun is used. Example: *Any* man or woman may enter *his* work in the contest. In colloquial English this is commonly handled by using a plural pronoun such as *their: Any man or woman may enter their work in the contest.* But this is an incorrect mismatch of a plural pronoun with a singular antecedent.

Rule 2: When the pronoun is followed by a prepositional phrase, the number of the pronoun is not affected. Look at the examples below:

1. *Each* of the cats left *its* [not *their*] paw prints on the car windshield.
2. *Anyone* in the class can bring *his* [not *their*] parents to the game for free.

Exception: *Some, all, any, most, none* may be singular or plural; this is determined by the sentence context, which is often found in the prepositional phrase that follows the pronoun.

1. *Some* of the cake lost *its* frosting. *None* of the boys lost *their* way.
2. *Any* girl may bring *her* handwork. *Any* class may bring *their* artwork.

Rule 3: When two (or more) singular antecedents are joined by *either/or* or *neither/nor*, a singular pronoun is used to refer to them. (This applies as well if they are joined simply by *or* or *nor*.)

N.B.

For common, singular antecedents, the masculine pronoun is generally used. Avoid the incorrect plural pronouns *they, them, their.*

Examples.

   Neither Ed nor John could reach *his* parents.
   Either Sue or Sally will turn in *her* paper first.

Rule 4: When two (or more) antecedents are joined by *and*, they are referred to by a plural pronoun. Example: Mr. and Mrs. Jones gave *their* land to the church.

Rule 5: When a relative pronoun (*who, which, that*) is used, its number is determined by its antecedent. Example: Anyone *who* wants to order pizza should raise *his* hand. The antecedent of *who* is *anyone. Anyone* is singular, requiring a singular pronoun.

EXERCISE A

Fill in the blank with an appropriate personal pronoun.

   1. After the concert, all of the students tried to get _____ programs signed by the performers.
   2. Either Eric or Mark will be selected to read _____ short story.
   3. Everyone in the college is expected to provide _____ own transportation.
   4. Every ballerina was at _____ bar.
   5. Each of the boarders has to do _____ own laundry.
   6. Several of the instructors brought _____ wives.
   7. Every choir member has _____ favorite piece.
   8. Nobody in the cab had brought _____ wallet.
   9. Katie and her sister were so late _____ father had begun to get worried.
   10. Both boys brought _____ luggage with them to the museum.
   11. If anyone calls while I am gone, please get _____ number.
   12. None of the boys was able to call _____ parents.
   13. Few of the preschoolers could tie _____ shoes.
   14. Neither runner ran _____ best in the relay.
   15. Robert and his brother bought _____ mountain bikes at the yard sale.
   16. Everyone demanded _____ opinion be heard.
   17. Neither Sue nor Tina ever answered _____ mail.
   18. If anyone wants a free ticket, _____ must call today.
   19. No one likes to find _____ uninvited. (himself, themselves)
   20. Neither of the baby birds could lift _____ wings.
   21. A young man must make it _____ aim to excel.
   22. Few of the dogs are obedient to _____ masters.

⌛ Historia

Aethelworld, Bishop of Winchester, is known for teaching Latin grammar using Anglo-Saxon. His most famous student was Aelfric, a monk born in the 950s and the author of the first known grammar written in English. It was a Latin grammar written in Anglo-Saxon (the West Saxon dialect) to help the English speaking people learn Latin. It included a discussion of the eight parts of speech and was much used in the eleventh century. Aelfric developed terms for grammar concepts in English and tried to explain Latin grammar through English. His work encouraged the study of grammar. Also called Grammaticus, he was considered one of the foremost prose writers of his time. He wrote many religious works, including an introduction to each of the testaments in the Bible, a work against transubstantiation (later published in 1566), and a dialogue or "Colloquy" between a teacher and his students. This is the only Anglo-Saxon work in which everyday, common topics are discussed. Aelfric contributed significantly to standardizing Anglo-Saxon vocabulary.

23. Some of the people were late to _____ appointments.

24. Emily or Laura will pick up _____ aunt and uncle at the airport.

Exercise B

Most of the following sentences have pronoun errors, either in agreement, case, or gender. Identify the incorrect pronoun(s) and write the correct one after it. If the sentence has no errors, write "correct."

1. Everyone brought their kite to the park.

2. Neither Mom nor her two sisters ever saw their parents again.

3. If anyone wants to join the class, they must sign up today.

4. Neither of the boys beat his own record on the team this year.

5. Each of the horses was looking his best at the race.

6. No one enjoys finding themself the only one who doesn't get the joke.

7. The staff awarded first place to Mary and I for our speech.

8. Several of the boys finished his assignment early.

9. Which of you girls will let me borrow their pen?

10. If any of you don't want to ride the bus, they can walk over to the park.

LESSON 37

REVIEW

EXERCISE A

Answer the following review questions.

1. What are the five categories of nouns?
2. What is number?
3. For what is the nominative case used?
4. What are the nominative case pronouns?
5. What case is used for the direct object?
6. English has what four genders?
7. What case is used to show ownership?
8. Name the case of each of these relative pronouns: *who, whom,* and *whose?*
9. What are the interrogative pronouns?
10. What is their function?
11. What are the singular demonstrative pronouns? Plural?
12. List as many of the indefinite pronouns as you can.
13. What are the two uses of the reflexive pronouns?

EXERCISE B

Write your own sentences using personal pronouns as directed below. Do not use *you* or *it.*

1. A sentence using personal pronouns as compound subjects in the sentence.
2. A sentence using a pronoun as a predicate nominative.
3. A sentence using a pronoun and a noun as compound direct objects.
4. A sentence using a pronoun and a noun as compound indirect objects.
5. A sentence using a pronoun and a noun as compound objects of the preposition.

UNIT FOUR

SPECIAL PROPERTIES OF VERBS

Verbs were briefly introduced in Lesson 2, but they are much more complicated and interesting than they first seem. Verbs express several things at once, including tense, voice, and mood, and they must agree with the person and number of their subjects. Verbs often change their form or take on helping verbs to express these things, but most verbs have only a few basic principal parts that are the models for all the different verb forms.

CONTENTS

THE PRINCIPAL PARTS OF A VERB

Explanation

Remember from Lesson 2 that **verbs** are the life of the sentence, the most important word (*verbum*) in any sentence. Verbs have five principal parts, and all the forms the verb can take come from these. The five principal parts of the verb are the **infinitive**, the **present**, the **past**, the **present participle**, and the **past participle**. We will look at each of these in detail below.

1. The **infinitive**: this is the form of the verb with *to* in front of it.

   Example. to bring, to jump, to sing (*to* + the verb)

2. The **present** form: this is the today form of the verb. It can also be used to express the future if *shall* or *will* is put in front of it.

   Examples. *bring, shall bring, will bring; jump, shall jump, will jump; sing, shall sing, will sing*

3. The **past** form: this is the yesterday form. It is often formed by the addition of *-ed* on the end, though not always.

   Examples. *brought, jumped, sang*

4. The **present participle**: this is the *-ing* form of the verb. It is used with some form of the helping verb *be*.

   Examples. *is bringing, is jumping, is singing*

5. The **past participle**: this form often follows a form of the helping verb *have*. It is used to conjugate all the perfect tenses of the verb and all of the passive voice.

   Examples. *has brought, have jumped, has sung*

Regular Verbs

A regular verb forms its past and past participle forms by simply adding *-ed* or *-d* to the infinitive form. They do not otherwise change their spelling.

■□ *Definition*
The *principal parts* of a verb represent the main forms it can take.

Infinitive	Present	Past	Pres. Participle	Past Participle
to work	work	work*ed*	working	(have) work*ed*
to walk	walk	walk*ed*	walking	(have) walk*ed*
to change	change	change*d*	changing	(have) change*d*

Irregular Verbs

The irregular verbs form their past and past participle by changing their spelling in various and unpredictable ways, or they do not change at all.

Infinitive	Present	Past	Pres. Participle	Past Participle
to begin	begin	began	beginning	(have) begun
to tear	tear	tore	tearing	(have) torn
to burst	burst	burst	bursting	(have) burst

✒ N. B.

When you look up an irregular verb in the dictionary, the past, past participle (if it is not the same as the past form), and present participle forms will be listed after the entry word in parentheses. Example: *sink* (sank or sunk, sunk or sunken, sinking).

EXERCISE A

The infinitive is given for the following verbs. List the other four principal parts of each.

to be	to write	to know
to drink	to steal	to ring
to come	to throw	to draw
to go	to take	to find
to swim	to fall	to make
to do	to give	to lay (put)
to blink	to drive	to lie (rest)
to bring	to speak	to have
to choose	to pay	to raise
to fly	to shrink	to rise
to see	to blow	
to eat	to sink	

LESSON 39

THE CONJUGATION OF VERBS

Verb forms change to show different times. English has six **tenses** or times expressed by verbs. Verbs have the power to show the time of the action (or condition) by means of **tense**.

1. **Present** tense is used to express what is occurring now, today, in the present. It is formed from the present principal part. Example: "She *runs* every morning."

2. **Past** tense expresses what occurred yesterday or sometime in the past, when it is not continuing into the present. This form of the verb comes from the past principal part. Example: "She *ran* yesterday."

3. **Future** tense expresses what is to come in the future. It uses the present form of the verb with the helping verb *shall* or *will*. Example: "She will run again." Though in our day *shall* and *will* have lost much of their distinctiveness, it is important that we remember the proper usage of each. These are the two rules governing the use of *shall* and *will*:

   a. To express the future, *shall* is used in the first person; *will* is used in the second and third persons. "I *shall* stay and listen." "*Shall* we go?" "You *will* win."

   b. In statements of promises, intentions, or obligations, *will* is used in the first person; *shall* is used in second and third persons. "I *will* keep my word." "He *shall* have my word on it."

4. **Present perfect** tense uses the past participle form with the helping verb *have* or *has*. It shows an action completed in the present time. Example: "She *has run.*"

5. **Past perfect** tense, like all the perfect tenses, is formed from the past participle. It requires the helping verb *had* and expresses an action that has been completed in the past. This is the earliest time expressed. Example: "She *had run.*"

N.B.

The **historical present** is used to make past events seem vivid and clear as though they are taking place in the present. For example, "Caesar lands in Britain in 55 B.C."

N.B.

Be sure to distinguish *shall* and *will*, and use them properly.

UNIT 4

6. **Future perfect** tense has *shall* or *will* as a helping verb (as future tense) plus *have* or *has*. It expresses an action as completed at some time in the future. It is formed from the past participle. Example: "She *will have run.*"

The Progressive Form

Although this is not a tense itself, each tense has this progressive form. This is simply the form taken when an action is asserted *in progress*. The present participle form is used for the progressive.

Present progressive: I am running.

Past progressive: I was running.

Future progressive: I shall be running.

Present perfect progressive: I have been running.

Past perfect progressive: I had been running.

Future perfect progressive: I shall have been running.

The Emphatic Form

Sometimes, in order to emphasize our point, to ask a question, or to express a negative statement, we use the **emphatic form**. The emphatic form is the infinitive (without the *to* in front of it) preceded by the helping verb *do*. Examples: I really *do like* it. I *don't want* to go. *Does* she *sing*? (We will not include the emphatic form in the conjugation below.)

Conjugation

To **conjugate** a verb is simply to list all the verb forms, in each tense, singular and plural, in all three persons. Consider the conjugation of the verb *sing* below.

Present infinitive: to sing   **Perfect infinitive:** to have sung

Principal Parts

Infinitive	*Present*	*Past*	*Pres. Participle*	*Past Participle*
to sing	sing(s)	sang	singing	(have) sung

Present Tense

Singular	*Plural*
I sing	we sing
you sing	you sing
He, she, it sings	they sing

Present progressive: I am singing, we are singing, you are singing, etc.

Past Tense

Singular	*Plural*
I sang	we sang
you sang	you sang
He, she, it sang	they sang

Past progressive: I was singing, we were singing, you were singing, etc.

Future Tense

Singular	*Plural*
I shall sing	we shall sing
you will sing	you will sing
He, she, it will sing	they will sing

Future progressive: I shall be singing, we shall be singing, you will be singing, etc.

Present Perfect Tense (*have* or *has* + the past participle)

Singular	*Plural*
I have sung	we have sung
you have sung	you have sung
He, she, it has sung	they have sung

Present perfect progressive: I have been singing, you have been singing, etc.

Past Perfect Tense (*had* + the past participle)

Singular	*Plural*
I had sung	we had sung
you had sung	you had sung
He, she, it had sung	they had sung

Past perfect progressive: I had been singing, we had been singing, you had been singing, etc.

Future Perfect Tense (*will have* or *shall have* + past participle)

Singular	*Plural*
I shall have sung	we shall have sung
you will have sung	you will have sung
He, she, it will have sung	they will have sung

Future perfect progressive: I shall have been singing, you will have been singing, etc.

EXERCISE

Select a verb of your choice and conjugate it on your own paper.

ACTIVE AND PASSIVE VOICE

Examples

1. **The tornado demolished the town.**

   The subject *tornado* performs the action. The verb is *demolished* and the direct object *town* receives the action, telling what was demolished.

2. **The town was demolished by the tornado.**

   In this revision of the sentence above, the object *town* has been moved to the position of subject. The verb has been changed from *demolished* to *was demolished*. The original subject *tornado* is now the object of the prepositional phrase.

Explanation

■□ *Definitions*

When the subject is performing the action of the verb, the verb is in the *active voice*. When the verb is acting upon the subject, the verb is in the *passive voice*.

When the subject of the sentence is doing the action expressed by the verb, as in sentence 1 above, the verb is in the **active voice**. When the action is performed on the subject so that the subject is the receiver, as in sentence 2, the verb is in the **passive voice**. A passive verb is formed from the past participle (principal part) and must always have one of the "to be" verbs as a helping verb. These include *am, are, is, was, were, be, being, been.*

EXERCISE A

Identify the italicized verbs in the sentences below as active or passive.

1. Eddie *grows* wheat on his farm in the Palouse.
2. His family *has farmed* the same land for three generations.
3. The land *has been plowed* and *planted* many times over the years.
4. Wheat *is planted* in the spring and fall.
5. Some years the farmers *harvest* the crop in early August.
6. Other years the crop *is harvested* in late August.
7. Heavy rains in late summer *can damage* the crop.

144

8. The crop *can* also *be damaged* by late spring frosts.

9. This year's crop *has* not *been harvested* yet.

10. Passive verbs *can be recognized* easily.

Exercise B

Rewrite the sentences below, changing the active voice to passive.

1. I admire her voice.
2. Tulips covered the hillside.
3. The wind destroyed my garden.
4. All the family enjoyed the barbecue.
5. I bought a new car last year.
6. The skier crossed the wake with ease.
7. He took a picture of the old bridge.
8. The boy mowed the lawn for his neighbor.
9. The toddler picked the raspberries and ate them.
10. The rain left puddles on the sidewalk.

✏ *N.B.*

The active voice is generally more powerful in writing. Too many passive sentences can weaken the overall effect of writing.

UNIT 4

Conjugating the Passive Voice Verb

Since we have already conjugated the active voice in the last lesson, we will conjugate the passive voice here. Remember that the past participle is used for the passive voice with the helping verb *to be*. Notice that the progressive form also uses the past participle.

Conjugation of the Verb *Call* in Passive Voice

Principal Parts

Infinitive	*Present*	*Past*	*Pres. Participle*	*Past Participle*
to call	call	called	calling	(have) called

Present Tense

Singular	*Plural*
I am called	we are called
you are called	you are called
He, she, it is called	they are called

Present progressive: I am being called

Past Tense

Singular	*Plural*
I was called	we were called
you were called	you were called
He, she, it was called	they were called

Past progressive: I was being called

Future Tense

Singular	*Plural*
I shall be called	we shall be called
you will be called	you will be called
He, she, it will be called	they will be called

Future progressive: I shall be being called

Present Perfect Tense

Singular	*Plural*
I have been called	we have been called
you have been called	you have been called
He, she, it has been called	they have been called

Present perfect progressive: I have been being called

Past Perfect Tense (*had* + the past participle)

Singular	*Plural*
I had been called	we had been called
you had been called	you had been called
He, she, it had been called	they had been called

Past perfect progressive: I had been being called

Future Perfect Tense (*will have* or *shall have* + past participle)

Singular	*Plural*
I shall have been called	we shall have been called
you will have been called	you will have been called
He, she, it will have been called	they will have been called

Future perfect progressive: I shall have been being called

Exercise C

Conjugate the verb *see* in the passive voice.

EXERCISE D

Write out the correct verb form with the necessary helping verbs.

1. First person, plural, future, passive of *to praise.*
2. Third person, singular, masculine, past, perfect active of *to sing.*
3. Second person, plural, present, passive of *to love.*
4. First person, singular, future perfect, passive of *to fly.*
5. Third person, plural, past, passive of *to see.*
6. Third person, singular, feminine, present, perfect passive of *to take.*
7. Third person, singular, neuter, past, passive of *to eat.*

LESSON 41

MOOD

Examples

1. **He is here. Is he here?**

   This example expresses a fact or asks a question.

2. **(you) Be here on time. Please be here on time.**

   This example expresses a command or request. The only helping verbs that can be used in this mode are the verbs *be* and *do*.

3. **Would that he were here on time.**

   This example expresses a wish, a doubt, an uncertainty, or a supposition, contrary to a fact. It is a mere thought.

Explanation

Mood simply means *manner* or *way*. The mood is the manner or way a verb expresses its action, being, or state. Though the study of mood is nearly obsolete in modern English grammar texts, it does still apply in the study of other languages. English has three moods: **indicative**, **imperative**, and **subjunctive**. The different moods are used to show how the thought in the sentence is presented. The word *mood* is used interchangeably with *mode*.

The **indicative** mood is the most common form of the verb and is used to make statements and ask questions. It is found in declarative and interrogative sentences. The **imperative** mood is found in the imperative sentence, but it is not limited to commands, for it includes requests as well. The **subjunctive** mood is used to imply condition, supposition, or uncertainty. Subjunctive means *joined under*; it is frequently used in dependent clauses.

■□ *Definitions*

Mood is the way in which a verb expresses its action, being, or state. The *indicative* mood makes statements or asks questions. The *imperative* mood is for commands and requests. The *subjunctive* mood implies condition, supposition, or uncertainty.

EXERCISE A

Identify the mood of the verbs in the following sentences.

1. In the day of prosperity be joyful, but in the day of adversity consider.

2. What profit has he who has labored for the wind?

3. Forgive us our trespasses.

4. Gather up the fragments that remain.

5. I would remain here if you wish.

6. He might improve, if he would make the effort.

7. Depart from me, you workers of iniquity.

8. Vanity of vanities, all is vanity.

9. Better is a poor and wise youth than an old and foolish king who will be admonished no more.

10. Fear God and keep His commandments, for this is the whole duty of man.

LESSON 42
TRANSITIVE AND INTRANSITIVE VERBS

Examples

1. The *hunter* spotted a *deer*.

   The action in this sentence is passing from the subject *hunter* to the object *deer*. In fact, without the object, the sentence would be incomplete.

2. **The *deer* was *spotted* by the hunter.**

   The action in this sentence is done upon the subject. No object is needed to complete the assertion of the verb.

Explanation

A **transitive verb** is one that cannot make a complete assertion (or a complete thought) without an object; it is incomplete without an object. The term *transitive* comes from the Latin meaning "to pass over." The action or feeling is passed over from the doer of the action (the subject) to an object on which the action falls. Only verbs that assert action can be transitive.

Look at sentence 1 above. *The hunter spotted* is not a complete thought. The object *deer* is needed to complete the assertion. An **intransitive verb** makes a complete assertion without an object. *Intransitive* simply means *not* transitive. Sentence 2 does not need an object to make a complete thought. **Action verbs** can be used as either transitive or intransitive verbs. In the sentence *She ran home*, *ran* is intransitive; in *She ran the race*, it is transitive.

Linking verbs do not express action. Instead they link the subject to the predicate nominative or predicate adjective. They are not classed as transitive or intransitive, but as linking verbs.

EXERCISE A

Identify the italicized verbs in the sentences below as transitive or intransitive.

1. Cain *killed* Abel.
2. John *wrote* a long letter to his brother.
3. God *made* the world.
4. She *wept*.
5. The bird *sat* very still on the branch.
6. She *heard* the clock ticking.
7. Bill *went* home for summer vacation.
8. Mother *closed* the door.
9. The child *loves* his mother.
10. The kite *rose* gracefully in the wind.

EXERCISE B

Compose two sentences using transitive verbs, two using intransitive verbs, and two using linking verbs.

EXERCISE C

In this excerpt from *Mrs. Wiggs of the Cabbage Patch* by Alice Caldwell Hegan, identify all the italicized verbs as transitive, intransitive, or linking. If a verb is transitive, underline the direct object.

1. After the curtain *descended* on the final tableau, Redding *waited* in the lobby while the stream of people *passed*.
2. The Wiggses *had obeyed* instructions, and *were* the very last to come out.
3. They *seemed* dazed by their recent glimpse into fairy-land.
4. Something in their thin bodies and pinched faces made Redding *form* a sudden resolve.
5. "Billy," he said gravely, "can't you and your family *take* supper with me?"
6. Billy and his mother *exchanged* doubtful glances.
7. For the past three hours everything *had been* so strange and unusual that they *were* bewildered.

⌛ Historia

Much of the early history of our language (from the Latin *lingua*, meaning *tongue*) is connected to war. The French conquered England in 1066 in what is often called the Norman Conquest. William the Conqueror won his decisive victory at the Battle of Hastings and became the King of England. The upper class learned Norman French, for it had become the language of the court and the aristocracy. Words were fused into the English language from French that had to do with government, military, art, dress, food, law, and the church. In the following three centuries, English gradually changed from an inflected language to a form closer to what it is today. Prepositions and helping verbs took the place of inflections. Word order in sentences became very important. As Normans intermarried with the English, the use of English in daily life gradually became the norm. By the end of the 1300s French influence had declined and English again became the language of choice in the court and in business. However, it was no longer the language that it had been, for it had picked up many new words from the French.

UNIT 4

LESSON 43

AGREEMENT OF SUBJECT AND VERB

Examples

1. Wendy *is* going to the movie with the students.

   The subject of the sentence is singular, and the verb is singular.
2. Wendy and Tom *are* going to the movie with the students.

   The subject of the sentence is plural, so the verb is plural.

Explanation

■□ *Definition*

Agreement of subject and verb means that they express the same number (singular or plural).

The verb must always agree with its subject in number. If the subject is singular, it must have a singular verb. Likewise, plural subjects take plural verbs. Below are some rules to govern subject-verb agreement. Some of these rules were covered in Lesson 36 (Pronoun Agreement).

1. If a prepositional phrase comes between the subject and the verb, the verb should still agree with the subject, not the object of the phrase.

   Examples:

   One *of the trees* is falling. Though the object of the preposition is plural, the subject is still singular.

   Samuel, *along with his sisters*, has decided to go to the library. Even if the prepositional phrase begins with *as well as* or *along with* or *in addition to*, the number of the subject is unaffected.
2. Remember the following pronouns are singular, so they require singular verbs: *each, either, neither, one, everyone, everybody, no one, nobody, anyone, anybody, someone, somebody.*

   Examples. Each of the boys was working quietly at his desk. Neither of my parents is going with me. Everyone in the class was late.
3. These pronouns are plural and require a plural verb: *several, both, many, few.*

   Examples. Both were on the plane. Few are coming.

4. These pronouns can take either a singular or plural verb, depending on the meaning of the sentence: *some, all, any, most, none.* The prepositional phrase that modifies the pronoun must be taken into account.

   Examples.

   > Some of the boys are going. All of the cars are red.
   > Some of the cake is missing. All of the gum is gone.
   > None of the toys are broken. Any of the boys are welcome.
   > None of the cake is left. Is any of the cake left?

5. A compound subject joined by *and* takes a plural verb.

   Examples. The letters and packages were left on the porch. Sue and Ted were invited to the wedding.

6. Sometimes compound subjects joined by *and* are still considered singular because we think of them as one thing.

   Examples. Peanut butter and jelly is my favorite kind of sandwich. Bacon and eggs is a great breakfast. Law and order has disintegrated.

7. Singular subjects joined by *or* or *nor* take a singular verb.

   Examples. Bob or Mary is coming to dinner. Neither Mom nor Dad knows I am home.

8. When a compound subject includes both a singular subject and a plural subject joined by *or* or *nor*, the verb must agree in number to the nearer one.

   Examples. Either the car or the trucks are responsible for the crash. Neither his sisters nor Bill wants to eat spaghetti tonight.

9. Collective nouns are either singular or plural. If the group is thought of as one unit, it is singular. If it is thought of as a collection of individuals acting separately, it is plural.

   Examples. The jury is undecided. The faculty were meeting to discuss their ideas for commencement.

10. Remember that the verb must agree with its subject, not the predicate nominative.

    Examples. The problem with his paper is the many grammatical errors. Birds are a problem in my garden.

11. When a sentence begins with *there* or *here*, be sure that the verb agrees with the subject. Be especially careful with the contractions *there's* and *here's*.

    Examples.

    > Here are my brothers. *Not* Here's my brothers.
    > There are the clothes you ordered. *Not* There's the clothes you ordered.

12. Amounts are usually considered singular.

   Examples. The ten dollars is missing. Three weeks is the length of the class. Twenty percent is too much.

13. When *every* or *many a* precedes a word or words, a singular verb is required.

   Examples. Every dandelion and thistle has been pulled up. Many a man, woman, and child has visited the Statue of Liberty.

14. The contractions *don't* and *doesn't* must agree in number with their subjects.

   Examples. She doesn't want to go. They don't want to go.

EXERCISE A

Select the appropriate verb to agree with the subject in the following sentences.

1. One of the students (is, are) presenting a paper today.
2. Sally, along with many classmates, (is, are) signed up for the field trip.
3. Nobody in the class (wants, want) to miss it.
4. Everyone in the neighborhood (was, were) at the picnic.
5. Few (was, were) tardy today.
6. Some of my aunt's dishes (is, are) broken.
7. Some of my uncle's tobacco (is, are) missing.
8. (Is, Are) any of you boys going to the gym?
9. (Is, Are) there any reason for this?
10. Law and order (is, are) the need of the hour.
11. Mr. Jones and Mr. Jacobs (was, were) absent from the board meeting.
12. (Is, Are) the salt and pepper on the table?
13. Neither hail nor sleet (was, were) expected.
14. Either the hall or the entryway (is, are) where I left the letter.
15. Either the dogs or the cat (is, are) making that noise.
16. The class (is, are) going skiing this weekend.
17. The cause of the destruction in my garden (is, are) the bunnies.
18. There (is, are) my cousins.
19. Six dollars (is, are) too much to pay.
20. Every car and bus (is, are) honking (its, their) horn.

LESSON 44

REVIEW

REVIEW QUESTIONS

1. Name the five principal parts of the verb.
2. What will the infinitive always have in front of it?
3. Which two principal parts will have helping verbs?
4. What is the difference between a regular and an irregular verb?
5. What are the principal parts of the verb *to swim*?
6. Name the six tenses.
7. What is unique about the third person singular present tense?
8. What helping verbs will the future tense always have?
9. What do the perfect tenses have in common?
10. The perfect tenses are formed from what principal part?
11. What is the progressive form?
12. What does it mean to conjugate a verb?
13. Define the active and passive voices.
14. Which will always have a helping verb?
15. Give the first person singular present tense of the active and passive voice of *to call*.
16. What is the difference between a transitive and an intransitive verb?
17. Transitive and intransitive verbs are two types of what kind of verb?
18. What are the two other types of verbs?
19. The verb must always agree with its subject in _____.
20. What if a prepositional phrase comes between the subject and the verb? Does the verb agree with the subject or the object of the preposition?
21. List ten pronouns that are always singular in number.
22. List four pronouns that are always plural in number.
23. Which five pronouns can take either a singular or a plural verb?
24. How do you determine which is required?

25. If the sentence has a compound subject joined by *and*, will the verb be singular or plural?

26. Why are some compound subjects joined by *and* (like *peanut butter and jelly*) considered singular?

27. Do singular subjects joined by *or* or *nor* take a singular or plural verb?

28. What is the rule for a compound subject that includes both a singular and a plural noun?

29. Explain the rule for collective nouns.

UNIT FIVE

VERBALS

Verbals are words that are formed from verbs but do not do the work of verbs. They act as other parts of speech. The three kinds of verbals are **participles**, **gerunds**, and **infinitives**. We will cover each in the next three lessons.

CONTENTS

LESSON 45

PARTICIPLES

Examples

1. The *growling* dog chased the postman down the street.
   Growling is part verb because it does include the action of growling. But it is also an adjective because it is describing the dog.
2. She woke the *sleeping* child and carried him into the house.
   The noun *child* is modified by the adjective *sleeping*. *Sleeping* is a verb form, but it is doing the work of an adjective.

Explanation

The **participle** is a verb doing the work of an adjective. It will always be formed from the present or past participle form. (Remember the principal parts of the verb from Lesson 38.) A participle with a helping verb will be a verb, as in *The dog was growling.* Without the helping verb the participle is an adjective. (Remember: the **present participle** is the *-ing* form of the verb as in the examples above. The **past participle** is the *-d* or *-ed* form of the verb.)

Examples. The *bruised* child was comforted by his mother. The rain fell on the *scorched* land.

Remember that some participles are irregular and will not end in *-d* or *-ed*.

Examples. The *burnt* toast made the house smell bad. The police returned the *stolen* silver.

> ■□ *Definition*
> A *participle* is a verb form that does the work of an adjective.

UNIT 5

Exercise A

Identify the participles in the sentences below and the noun each modifies.

1. We gave him an illustrated dinosaur book for his birthday.
2. The winding road led to our grandparents' home.
3. She hired a contractor to repair the damaged roof.

159

4. He wanted to grow up to become a wandering minstrel.

5. Migrating geese fly over our house each fall.

6. The yelping puppies tumbled out the door to greet our visitors.

7. The teacher addressed the assembled class.

8. My disappointed daughter held back her tears.

9. The exhausted relay team collapsed in the shade.

10. She looked with curiosity at the forbidden box.

The Participial Phrase

■□ *Definition*

A *participial phrase* is a participle along with its modifiers and complements. The whole phrase acts like an adjective.

A participle can have modifiers or complements. Like any adjective, the participle can be modified by an adverb or a prepositional phrase used as an adverb. The entire group of related words acts together as an adjective and is called a **participial phrase**.

Examples.

1. *Spying the house*, the salesman quickened his pace. This participial phrase includes a direct object, *house*. The entire phrase modifies *salesman*.

2. I could see the children *swinging in the tree*. The participial phrase includes an adverbial prepositional phrase *in the tree*.

3. *Ushered quickly to our seats*, we were relieved the show had not yet begun. The participle *ushered* is modified by the adverb *quickly* and the prepositional phrase *to our seats*.

▼ *Punctuation Note*

Participial phrases require commas when they come at the beginning of the sentence, or if they are not essential to the meaning of the sentence.

Participial phrases sometimes require commas. These are the simple rules:

1. When a participial phrase begins a sentence, it is always followed by a comma, as in the sample sentences 1 and 3 above.

2. When a participial phrase comes in the middle of the sentence, it is surrounded by commas if it is not essential to the meaning of the sentence. (This is the same rule that governs the use of commas around an adjective clause.) If the participial phrase is essential, no commas are needed.

3. A participial phrase at the end of a sentence needs no commas, as in sentence 2 above.

EXERCISE B

Find the participial phrases in the following sentences:

1. The team, tired from the heat, finally won the championship game.
2. Leading at half-time, the team had felt confident.
3. The top scorer, acclaimed for his quickness, suffered an injury soon after the half.
4. The rest of the team, wearied from several previous games, knew they had to work harder.
5. Plagued by more injuries and poor shots, the team almost lost.

Diagraming

The participle is written around the curve of a bent line under the word it modifies. (Notice the line has no tail.) Any of its modifiers are placed under it, and any complements are placed beside it appropriately.

Examples:

1. *Spying the house, the salesman quickened his pace.*

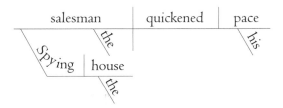

2. *I could see the children swinging in the tree.*

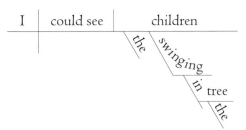

⌛ *Historia*

William Caxton (1421-91), the first English printer, often included apologies for the poor state of the English language in his introductions to the translations he printed. He used words like *common*, *imperfect*, and *rude* to describe English. However, he thought Chaucer improved the language in the lovely style of *The Canterbury Tales*. Other writers like Spenser and Sidney made English acceptable and approved as equal to other written languages, but Latin was still considered above comparison—the perfect language. The English people had such reverence for the classical languages that they thought they should imitate Latin in everything. For example, because English poetry did not use hexameters like Latin poetry, it was thought to be inferior and deficient. By the eighteenth century, Greek was thought to be the purest language on earth and Latin was considered a corrupt form of Greek. The romance languages were considered "vulgar dialects" or corruptions of Latin. As men were working to create rules to govern English grammar, they turned to Greek and Latin as models. If a certain grammatical construction could not be found in Latin, it was considered to be illogical and therefore should not be tolerated in English. In reaction to this, other grammarians arose to contest the heavy reliance on the Latin model. Though in the end Latin was abandoned as a model for English, we still have many evidences of the early preoccupation with Latin in our modern grammar.

UNIT 5

3. *Ushered quickly to our seats, we were relieved the show had not yet begun.*

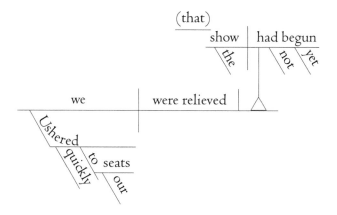

Exercise C

Diagram the sentences below. Some have more than one participle.

1. The singing choir marched onto the stage.
2. Scaling the wall, the convict nearly escaped.
3. Offering her his hand, he helped her from the car.
4. Seeing the large crowd gathered for the occasion, the speaker almost lost his nerve.
5. Annoyed at her own clumsiness, the rider got back on the frightened horse.

Dangling Participles

■▢ Definition
A *dangling participle* or participial phrase is not positioned next to the word it modifies and thus appears to be modifying a different word.

Notice in all the sentences above, the participle or participial phrase is located next to the word it modifies. Placement of the phrase will affect the meaning of the sentence. Consider this example:

Version 1: I could see the children *swinging in the tree.* (The participial phrase modifies *children.*)
Version 2: *Swinging in the tree,* I could see the children. (The participial phrase modifies *I.*)

Sometimes the result is confusion, as in the following sentence:

Version 1: The huge truck *loaded with timber* slid off the road and into a gas station. (*Truck* is modified.)

Version 2: The huge truck slid off the road and into a gas station *loaded with timber*. (*Station* is modified.)

Exercise D

Form the present and past participles of each of the verbs below, and write a sentence using each to modify nouns or pronouns.

Example. Think, thinking, thought: *Thinking* absentmindedly, the man missed his bus. *Thought* a failure, the musical was canceled.

1. See
2. Speak
3. Weave
4. Burn
5. Grow

Exercise E

Rewrite the sentences below correcting any dangling modifiers.

1. The huge tree finally gave way to the fierce wind swaying dangerously.
2. Spinning his web, the little boy was intrigued by the spider.
3. Rising above the hills, we saw the moon just before midnight.
4. We sometimes lose our sense of duty insisting on our rights.
5. Screaming and chattering, we saw the blue jay in its nest.

LESSON 46

GERUNDS

Examples

1. She loves *running*.

   Running is a verb form doing the work of a noun. *Running* is the direct object.

2. *Biting* your nails is an unwise habit.

   In this sentence the verb form *biting* has an object, *nails*. The whole phrase *biting your nails* is the subject of the sentence.

3. She improved her health by *losing* twenty-five pounds.

   Losing is a verb form used as the object of the preposition. It has an object, *pounds*.

Explanation

■☐ *Definition*

A *gerund* is a present participle verb form used as a noun.

Some present participles do the work of nouns as the subject, direct object, or object of the preposition in a sentence. (Remember the present participle always ends in *-ing*.) These verb forms are called **gerunds**.

EXERCISE A

Identify the gerunds in the following sentences.

1. Bobbing for apples is an old-fashioned fall pastime.
2. He won by running the last lap full speed.
3. Swinging makes her dizzy.
4. The people love the preaching at that church.
5. The doctor's chief concern is her erratic breathing.

The Gerund Phrase

The gerund can have modifiers and complements, just like any other noun. A **gerund phrase** includes the gerund and all its modifiers or complements. The entire phrase acts together as a noun.

Example. *Autographing books after his lectures* is one of his pet peeves. (The whole italized phrase is the subject.)

Exercise B

Identify the gerunds or gerund phrases in the following sentences and state how they are used in the sentence (subject, direct object, indirect object, object of the preposition, predicate nominative, appositive).

1. My mother delights in baking cookies for her grandchildren.
2. Cleaning the oven is not my favorite task.
3. By printing a retraction, the error was corrected.
4. Forgiving those who wrong you may be difficult, but it is necessary.
5. Something that I have always enjoyed is hanging wallpaper.
6. My vacation last year, visiting my aunt in Hawaii, will be hard to top.
7. By gossiping about her friends, she has created much havoc.
8. I dislike playing the accordion.
9. Listening to the clock chime is a joy to my grandson.
10. She loves surfing and scuba diving in the summer.

■☐ *Definition*

A *gerund phrase* is a gerund along with its modifiers and complements. The whole phrase acts as a noun.

UNIT 5

Diagraming

The gerund is placed on a stair-stepped platform on stilts. The stilts touch the line where the noun belongs. All modifiers and complements are placed accordingly.

Example. She loves decorating the house for Christmas.

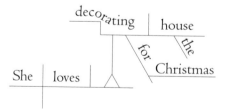

Exercise C

Diagram the following sentences.

1. He earned money during the summer by mowing lawns.
2. His latest hobby is collecting old coins.
3. Painting old furniture is her full-time job.
4. The children love singing in the church choir.
5. Her assignment, writing several poems, was both difficult and enjoyable.

LESSON 47

INFINITIVES

Examples

1. *To hit* a home run is his dream.

   The subject of the sentence is *to hit*. *To hit* has an object, *home run*. *To hit* is a noun.

2. **The print in this old book is hard** *to read.*

   To read is an adverb modifying the adjective *hard*.

3. **This is the place** *to be.*

   To be is modifying *place* and is an adjective.

Explanation

The **infinitive** is the simple, base form of the verb. When we refer to a verb, we speak of the infinitive form. The sign of the infinitive is the word *to* preceding the verb. The infinitive can be used as an **adjective**, an **adverb**, or a **noun**. *Infinitive* means *infinite* or *unlimited*. This is appropriate because the **infinitive** has many uses, and it is not affected by the number or person of the nouns and pronouns that are used with it. Remember, *to* plus a noun or a pronoun is a prepositional phrase.

■☐ *Definition*

An *infinitive* is a verb form, usually preceded by the word *to*, that is used as a noun, an adjective, or an adverb.

UNIT 5

EXERCISE A

Identify the infinitives and how each is used (as noun, adjective, or adverb) in the following sentences. Some sentences may have two.

1. This is weather to watch carefully.
2. I want to learn to skate.
3. The young boy tried to read the sign.
4. The plane is ready to take off.
5. The mechanic to call is Pete.

6. I want to tell you the truth.

7. Learn to do good.

8. To obey is better than sacrifice.

9. They are in a hurry to leave.

10. That was a day to remember.

The Infinitive Phrase

■□ *Definition*

An *infinitive phrase* is an infinitive along with its modifiers and complements.

Like other verbals, the infinitive phrase can have its own complements and modifiers to make it an **infinitive phrase**. The entire phrase is used as a single part of speech: a noun, an adjective, or an adverb.

Example. *To cruise down the Mississippi on a steamboat* is my dream vacation for next spring. (The infinitive phrase is a noun used as the subject.)

Exercise B

Identify the infinitives or infinitive phrases in the following sentences. Also state whether the infinitive is used as a noun, an adjective, or an adverb. If it is a noun, tell how it is used in the sentence.

1. She is a pleasure to know.

2. We are excited to go on our trip.

3. This salsa is too hot for me!

4. To succeed, you must work hard.

5. I like to spend my vacation time at home.

6. She is hoping to pass her test.

7. The boys are ready to go.

8. The baby in the tub is so fun to watch.

9. To find the time to exercise is hard for me.

10. Do you want to go to the show with me?

Diagraming

The infinitive is also diagramed on stilts above the base line. The *to* is always put on the slanted line and the verb on the horizontal line.

Example. I am hoping to see my grandparents in the summer.

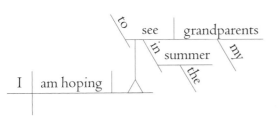

Historia

With the invention of the printing press, English began to become more rigid. The growing number of printed books and a populace able to read and write made the language more able to resist change. While it was only a spoken language, it was far more fluid and malleable. In the last four hundred years English has changed very little. You can see this by reading the King James Version of the Bible. Though some archaic words appear, the language is easily recognizable as English! Still, new words do continue to come in, and old words, forms, and uses change. We continue to borrow words from other languages, but today it is far more common for foreign countries to borrow words from English.

Infinitive Notes

1. **Sometimes the *to* in the infinitive is omitted.** This happens commonly after the following verbs: *please, see, hear, feel, watch, help, know, dare, need, make,* and *let.* **Examples.** The boys helped (to) carry the sick man inside. She didn't dare (to) go in late.

2. **The infinitive can have a subject.** An infinitive with a subject is sometimes called an *infinitive clause.*
   Examples. My parents asked him to sing at the reception. (The subject of *to sing* is *him.*) Did you see him (to) run that lap? (The subject of the infinitive *to run* is *him.*) I watched her (to) win the race. (The subject of the infinitive *to win* is *her.*)

3. **The pronoun subject of an infinitive is in the objective case** (*him, her,* etc.). The sample diagram below includes an infinitive with a subject and an omitted *to.*
   Example. I watched her win the race.

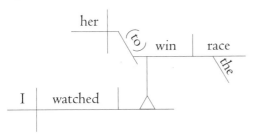

Exercise C
Diagram the following sentences with infinitive phrases.
1. Take time to do well.
2. To do well is not easy for the lazy.
3. It is hard for them to have a thankless child.

4. She used to study classics at Oxford before she moved to the States to teach.

5. He has the ability to win the race.

Infinitive Errors

1. **The Split Infinitive:** To split an infinitive is to place a modifier between the *to* and the verb.

   Example. Incorrect: I hoped to *never* see him again. Correct: I hoped never to see him again.

   This practice is not as objectionable as it once was; however, it should be avoided when possible. From Fowler's *Modern English Usage*: "We maintain, however, that a real s.i., though not desirable in itself, is preferable to either of two things, to real ambiguity, and to patent artificiality."

2. **Dropping the Verb:** *To* should not be used alone without the verb following.

   Example. Are we picking up Susie?

   Incorrect: She asked me *to*. Correct: She asked me *to give* her a ride.

3. **Sometimes *and* is substituted for *to*.** This is a subtle one. Depending on the meaning of the sentence, it may be incorrect.

   Examples. Try *to* come for lunch on Tuesday. Try *and* come for lunch on Tuesday.

REVIEW EXERCISE

Diagram the following sentences with verbals.

1. Racing down the hill, I tried to catch the runaway pony, but he disappeared into the woods before I could reach him.

2. The disappointed crowd is hoping to see the show if the audio can be repaired.

3. Believing that elves and fairies lived in these hills was once common among the plain folk.

UNIT SIX

THE SPECIAL PROPERTIES OF MODIFIERS

Nouns and verbs aren't the only parts of speech that have changing forms and more complicated aspects. Adjectives and adverbs can both modify a noun and compare it to other nouns at the same time. They have three basic forms that express **degree: positive, comparative,** and **superlative**.

CONTENTS

ADJECTIVES AND ADVERBS, COMPARATIVE AND SUPERLATIVE

Examples

1. Your poem is *short*.

   The adjective *short* describes the poem without comparing it to other poems.
2. This poem is *shorter* than yours.

   This poem has more *shortness* than the poem in sentence 1.
3. Mary's poem is the *shortest* in the class.

   Here the poem is compared to all others in the group. It has the greatest degree of *shortness.*

Explanation

■❏ *Definitions*

The *positive degree* expresses a state without making comparisons. The *comparative degree* places one thing in comparison with others. The *superlative degree* states that one thing is of a higher or lower degree than others.

Adjectives and adverbs show comparison of degrees of quantity or quality. There are three degrees of comparison: positive, comparative, superlative. The **positive** degree expresses the simple state of the quantity or quality, as in *good, wise, fast, tall.* The **comparative** degree expresses that one object, as compared to one other, has a higher or lower degree of quality or quantity, as in *better, wiser, less wise, faster, taller.* The **superlative** degree expresses that one of several objects has a higher or lower degree of quality or quantity than any of the others, as in *best, wisest, least wise, fastest, tallest.*

Rules for Forming Comparison

1. Adjectives and adverbs of one syllable commonly form their comparative by adding *r* or *er* to the positive, as *wise, wiser; great, greater; fast, faster.* They form the superlative by adding *st* or *est*, as *wise, wisest; great, greatest; fast, fastest.*
2. Adjectives and adverbs of two syllables form their comparative and superlative by either adding *er* and *est* or by prefixing *more* and *most* to the positive.

Generally, *more* and *most* are used to prevent awkward sounding words. Some modifiers of two syllables can use both forms, *er* and *est* as well as *more* and *most*, as, *handsome, handsomer, handsomest; more handsome, most handsome*. Adding *er* and *est* sometimes affects the spelling of the positive, as *blue, bluer; red, redder; happy, happier*.

3. Modifiers of more than two syllables form the superlative by prefixing *more* and *most* to the positive, as *beautiful, more beautiful, most beautiful; generous, more generous, most generous*.

4. Diminution of quality or quantity is expressed by prefixing *less* and *least* before the positive, as *bold, less bold, least bold*.

Irregular Comparison

Those modifiers that do not form their comparative and superlative in the regular way are called irregular. A dictionary will list the comparative and superlative forms after the word entry in parentheses if they are formed irregularly. Below are some of those that are compared irregularly.

Positive	Comparative	Superlative
good, well	better	best
bad, evil, ill	worse	worst
far	farther, further	farthest, furthest
little	less	least
many, much	more	most
old	older, elder	oldest, eldest

N.B.

Some adjectives form their superlative by suffixing *most* to the comparative or to the positive. *Up, upper, uppermost; in, inner, innermost; hind, hinder, hindmost; far, further, furthermost.* Some modifiers cannot be compared at all. These include *square, first, wooden, daily, infinite.* Though technically some words should not be comparable, they commonly are. This would include *perfect, more perfect, less perfect, most perfect, least perfect; complete, more complete, most complete.*

Comparison Errors

1. Use the word *other* or *else* when the thing being compared is part of the comparison group.
   Example. Craig is taller than anyone on the team. Since Craig is on the team, he cannot be taller than himself. *Correct:* Craig is taller than anyone else on the team *or* Craig is taller than any other boy on the team.

2. Do not use both the *er* or *est* ending and *more* or *most*. This is a double comparison.

UNIT 6

⏳ *Historia*

The story of how we got our punctuation is a tangled one. In Anglo-Saxon writings punctuation is erratic. The period and the semicolon are used interchangeably, probably more for rhetorical effect or to signal a pause for breathing rather than for grammatical reasons. Capitals were used at the beginning of sentences or important clauses as well as for names of some people. In the Middle English period a variety of punctuation appears in Chaucer's *Canterbury Tales*. A slash is used at the end of phrases, periods appear occasionally; inverted semicolons, groups of dots, and what may be question marks also appear. These marks were probably used to assist in reading the passages aloud. Abbreviations are sometimes, but not always, used for words like *with* and *that*, and capitals are used only with some proper nouns. In Middle English a full stop was indicated not by a period but by a plus sign or a group of dots. It was not until the sixteenth century that the apostrophe was used to indicate a missing letter. It was during this time that the semicolon became popular and was used interchangeably with the colon. The question mark was used both for questions and exclamations, and double commas were used to designate speech. Printers in the seventeenth century used italics, different kinds of font, asterisks, and pointing fingers for emphasis. One thing is certain: there was no consistency in punctuation.

Example. *Incorrect:* She is more friendlier than she used to be. *Correct:* She is more friendly than she used to be.

3. Be clear and not confusing.

Examples. I like bagels more than you. (The sentence is ambiguous: I like bagels more than you like bagels *or* I like bagels more than I like you.) *Incorrect:* Riding on a motorcycle is more dangerous than a car. *Correct:* Riding on a motorcycle is more dangerous than riding in a car.

4. Do not use the superlative to compare two objects.

Example. *Incorrect:* He is the youngest of the two. *Correct:* He is the younger of the two.

EXERCISE A

Form the comparative and superlative for the following modifiers. If a modifier cannot be compared, leave blank.

Positive	Comparative	Superlative
good	_____	_____
rich	_____	_____
virtuous	_____	_____
boiling	_____	_____
destructive	_____	_____
straight	_____	_____
round	_____	_____
strong	_____	_____
robust	_____	_____
sincere	_____	_____
low	_____	_____
swift	_____	_____
grateful	_____	_____
studious	_____	_____
little	_____	_____
extensive	_____	_____
slowly	_____	_____
rapid	_____	_____
soon	_____	_____
sweetly	_____	_____
merry	_____	_____
brilliant	_____	_____
white	_____	_____

EXERCISE B

Underline the adjectives or adverbs in the sentences below and state the degree of comparison of each.

1. Tomorrow promises to be the most glorious day.
2. The sun is more brilliant than the moon.
3. That was the best rehearsal so far.
4. What a merry little tune that was.
5. The shadows are growing longer.

EXERCISE C

Some of the sentences below contain comparison errors. Rewrite the sentence with corrections or write *C* if the sentence is correct.

1. Which of the two books do you like best?
2. The yard looks more lovelier than it ever has before.
3. I prefer eating at Swilly's than Bonanza.
4. This is the shortest haircut I've ever had.
5. This book is older than all the books in the library.

DANGLING OR MISPLACED MODIFIERS

Examples

1. **Throw the cow out the window some hay.**

   The wrong word (*cow*) is used as the direct object.

   The adverb phrase *out the window* is misplaced.

   Throw some hay out the window to the cow. Throw the cow some hay.

2. **I heard the President speaking in history class to Congress.**

   The adverb phrase *in history class* is misplaced.

   In history class I heard that the President was speaking to Congress.

   In history class we listened to the radio broadcast of the President addressing Congress.

3. **Riding in the back seat of the car, the radio drowned out the conversation.**

   The dangling participial phrase appears to be modifying *radio*.

   Riding in the back seat of the car, I could not hear the conversation.

Explanation

Each of the sentences above is confusing due to an error in the placement of a single word, a phrase, or a clause, or because of an omission of some kind. To keep writing clear, all modifiers must be placed as close as possible to the words they modify.

Exercise

Rewrite the following sentences correcting misplaced or dangling modifiers. Words may need to be added to make the sentences clear.

1. She wanted to bake cookies for the party with frosting and sprinkles.
2. While practicing the trumpet, the neighbor's dog began howling.
3. Having driven several blocks, the tailgate flew open.
4. I almost ran over the woman with her poodle in the large hat.
5. While baking the bread, the house smelled good.

PUNCTUATION APPENDIX

Punctuation is designed to be a help to our written communication. Too much as well as too little punctuation can be a hindrance to our writing. In many cases it is the author's call whether a comma is needed or not. Is this clause essential or nonessential? One author declared, "I spent all morning putting in a comma and all afternoon taking it out." Our writing should be clear and easily understood. A good use of punctuation keeps the reader from tripping up and having to go back to reread a sentence in order to understand it.

This appendix is designed to broadly cover the most common uses of punctuation. For editing or writing technical or research papers, or for help with the finer points of punctuation, I recommend you consult a style manual. Every student should have at least one on his shelf to help untangle the varied difficulties that can arise.

Capital Letters

Let me quote the esteemed Fowler: "If there is method here, it is hard to discern it. Let it be repeated: the employment of capitals is a matter not of rules but of taste; but consistency is at least not a mark of bad taste."*

1. The first word of every sentence or quotation always begins with a capital letter.
2. Proper nouns are always capitalized. This includes the following:
   * Names of persons
   * Geographical names

* H. W. Fowler, *A Dictionary of Modern English Usage*, 2nd ed. (Oxford: Oxford Univ. Press, 1965), 75.

- Names of organizations, clubs, business firms, institutions, buildings, government bodies
- Historical events and periods, special events, calendar items (days, months, holidays)
- Nationalities, races, religions
- Brand names
- Names of ships, trains, planes, etc.
- Names of heavenly bodies (planets, stars, etc.), but not *sun, moon,* or *earth* (unless they appear in a list where the others are all capitalized)
- Full titles or ranks of persons when appearing before a name
- Titles alone if referring to a high official, as the President of the United States
- Titles of literary works, movies, paintings, etc. (first, last, and all important words in the title)
- All words referring to God (*Lord, Father,* as well as the pronouns *He, Him, His*)

3. Proper adjectives are capitalized, as *Latin, French,* etc.
4. The pronoun *I* and the interjection *O* are always capitalized, as "I will love you, O Lord, my strength" (Psalm 18:1).

End Marks

The Period

A declarative or imperative sentence is closed with a period. Periods are also used after abbreviations.

The Question Mark

An interrogative sentence is closed with a question mark.

The Exclamation Point

The exclamation point must be used with care, for too many can give the reader the impression that the writer is "yelling" in print. As Fowler says, "Excessive use of exclamation marks is . . . one of the things that betray the uneducated or unpractised writer."* However, not to use an exclamation mark

* Ibid., 590.

when it is required is also incorrect. An exclamatory sentence is closed with an exclamation point.

If an imperative is uttered with strong emotion, it may be closed with an exclamation point, as *Shut the door!* A single word or phrase used as an interjection is followed by an exclamation point.

The Comma

Some writers just insert a comma whenever they feel the need to breathe. Although many of their instincts may be correct, it is better to know exactly why a comma is needed. Do not use a comma unless there is a good reason for it. Too many commas can be worse than too few.

1. Commas are used to separate elements in a series.
    a. When more than one adjective, adverb, or phrase is modifying the same word, commas are used to separate them. *The old, tall, red maple tree was blown over in the storm.* A comma separates the adjectives *old, tall,* and *red maple* from the noun *tree.* However, no comma is needed between *red* and *maple* because the word *maple* is commonly associated with the word *tree.* We use commas to keep things clear. If the adjectives are separated by *and,* no punctuation is needed: *The day was bright and sunny and warm.*
    b. A series of prepositional, introductory phrases requires a comma.
    c. A series of short, independent clauses is separated by commas.
2. Commas are used to separate clauses and participial phrases.
    a. A comma is used before the conjunction joining independent clauses. Be careful you do not confuse a sentence with a compound verb with a compound sentence. Do not use a comma between compound verbs.
    b. Nonessential adjective clauses are enclosed in commas.
    c. An introductory adverb clause is always followed by a comma. Adverb clauses, when they appear in the middle of the sentence, are enclosed in commas. No comma is needed when it comes at the end of the sentence.
    d. When a participial phrase begins a sentence, it is always followed by a comma. When it appears in the middle of the sentence, it is surrounded by commas if it is nonessential to the meaning of the sentence. A participial phrase at the end of a sentence needs no commas.
3. Commas are used with various interrupters.

a. The appositive or appositive phrase is set off from the other parts of the sentence by commas unless the appositive is a single word closely connected to the word it explains.

b. Words used to address a person directly are set off with commas. *You, my friend, are quite wrong. Mom, I'm home.* This word of direct address is called the *vocative*, from the Latin *voco*, meaning *I call*.

c. Expressions used as parenthetical comments or asides are set off by commas. Some of these common expressions include *to tell the truth, in my opinion, on the other hand, for example, however, nevertheless, in fact, of course, on the contrary*, etc.

4. The comma has many other uses.

a. Dates: A comma separates the day and the year. In a sentence with a specific date listed, a comma also follows the year. *On July 29, 1917, my father was born.*

b. Addresses: When listing someone's address, a comma follows the name, street, and town. *Mrs. Jill Brown, 2524 Mountain Road, Chesapeake City, Maryland 00196.* On the envelope a comma is placed between the city and state.

c. A comma is placed in a friendly letter after the salutation *(Dear Dan,)* and after the closing *(Yours truly,)* in both a friendly or business letter. The salutation in a business letter is followed by a colon.

d. A comma is also used after a name when it is followed by Jr., Sr., or by Ph.D., M.A., or other titles or degrees.

The Semicolon

1. A semicolon may be used between closely related independent clauses in place of a comma (used with a conjunction) or a period.

a. We were glad it snowed all day, for it cheered us to see the lovely white cover up the brown hills.

b. We were glad it snowed all day. It cheered us to see the lovely white cover up the brown hills.

c. We were glad it snowed all day; it cheered us to see the lovely white cover up the brown hills.

2. A semicolon is used between independent clauses that are joined by words such as *therefore, however, nevertheless, consequently, for instance, for example, accordingly, besides, moreover.*

We bought our tickets early; however, we still had to wait in line.

3. If the independent clauses already contain commas, it is better to separate them with a semicolon than with another comma. Too many commas can be confusing. *My daughter, rising characteristically late, took a long, leisurely bath; but finding it made her tired, she had to take a nap.*

4. A semicolon is used between the items in a series if the items themselves contain commas. *The winners were Scott Smith, first grade; Sally Anderson, second grade; and Beth Williams, third grade.*

The Colon

1. A colon directs attention to what follows after it. It is used before a series of items but should not follow a verb or a preposition. It may be used after *as follows* or *the following.*

2. A colon may be used before a long quotation.

3. Other uses include the following:

   a. Between the hour and minute in writing the time.

   b. Between the chapter and verse when citing a Scripture verse.

   c. After the salutation in a business letter.

Italics or Underlining

1. Italics are used for titles of books, magazines and journals, works of art, musical compositions, names of ships, planes, trains, etc.

2. The Bible and the names of books in the Bible are not italicized, underlined, nor put in quotation marks.

3 Italics are used for words or letters when they are referred to as such: "Don't forget to cross your *t*'s and dot your *i*'s."

4. Italics are used for foreign words.

Quotation Marks and Commas

1. Quotation marks are used for titles of short stories, articles, short poems, songs, and chapters of books.

2. Quotation marks are used at the beginning and end of a direct quotation.

3. When a quotation is divided by an interrupter like *he replied,* the second part of the quotation is not capitalized, and the interrupter is surrounded by commas. *"What," said Bob, "is the problem?"*

4. If the quotation is a question or exclamation, no comma is needed between the quotation and the reference to the speaker. *"Where are you going?" asked Mom.*

5. In a quotation of more than one paragraph, no quotation marks are used at the end of the first paragraph. Each new paragraph begins with quotation marks, and the final paragraph is closed with quotation marks. (See the example below the next rule.)

6. Single quotation marks are used for a quotation within a quotation. If a series of quotations are laced within quotations, single and double quotation marks are alternated.

> *"You have heard that it was said, 'You shall love your neighbor and hate your enemy.' But I tell you not to resist an evil person. But whoever slaps you on your right cheek, turn the other to him also.*
>
> *"If anyone wants to sue you and take away your tunic, let him have your cloak also. And whoever compels you to go one mile, go with him two.*
>
> *"Give to him who asks you, and from him who wants to borrow from you do not turn away."*

7. Periods and commas are always placed inside the end quotation marks. Colons and semicolons are placed outside the end quotation marks. Other punctuation marks are placed according to their use: if they punctuate the quotation, they are placed inside; if they punctuate the sentence in which the quotation appears, they are placed outside. Sometimes, as in the second example below, the quotation and the sentence each require a punctuation mark. *"Where were you all afternoon?" the man asked his secretary. Did you say, "Will you marry me?"?*

8. In dialogue a new paragraph is used for each change of speaker. Any descriptive or narrative material may be placed in the same paragraph if it relates to the speaker.

9. When two characters are speaking back and forth, it is not necessary to identify the speaker with each quotation.

The Dash

The dash is used to indicate a sharp break in thought.

> *If the snow continues—and we have no idea if it will—the conference will have to be canceled.*